FREEDOM FROM AVOIDANT ATTACHMENT

TRANSFORM AVOIDANCE INTO CONNECTION BY UNDERSTANDING DISMISSIVE PATTERNS, IDENTIFYING TRIGGERS, AND BUILDING A SECURE RELATIONSHIP

ELIZA BENNETT

CONTENTS

Introduction   vii

1. UNDERSTANDING AVOIDANT ATTACHMENT   1
   The Roots of Avoidant Attachment: Childhood
   Wounds and Early Experiences   2
   Identifying Dismissive Patterns   4
   The Impact on Personal Relationships   6
   Avoidant Attachment in Professional Settings   9
   Self-Reflection: Recognizing Your Attachment Style   11

2. DEEPER UNDERSTANDING AND AWARENESS OF
   AVOIDANT ATTACHMENT   17
   Understanding Your Core Wounds   17
   Identifying Emotional Triggers   19
   Building Emotional Self-Awareness   21
   Understanding Avoidant Behaviors in Conflict   23
   Overcoming Fear of Intimacy   26
   Understanding Shame and Self-Worth   28
   Somatic Awareness and Healing   31

3. CULTURAL AND GLOBAL CONTEXTS OF
   ATTACHMENT   33
   Understanding Cultural Attachment Variations   34
   Embracing Diversity in Attachment Styles   37
   Cross-Cultural Relationship Dynamics   40
   Respecting Cultural Variations in Attachment   42
   Inclusive Strategies for a Global Community   45

4. BRIDGING AWARENESS AND CHANGE   49
   Implementing Sustainable Change   50
   Managing Resistance and Setbacks   51
   Creating Lasting Transformation   52
   Integration and Ongoing Growth   53

5. TRANSFORMING AVOIDANT PATTERNS
   THROUGH TRUST AND EMOTIONAL INTIMACY   55
   Foundation of Trust After Avoidance   55
   Initial Steps in Emotional Connection   59
   Developing Healthy Communication Skills   62
   Managing Emotional Detachment   65
   Embracing Vulnerability in Relationships   67

6. BUILDING SECURE ATTACHMENTS   71
   Foundations of Secure Attachment   72
   Cultivating a Secure Attachment Mindset   74
   Advancing Trust in Secure Relationships   77
   Mastering Deep Emotional Connection   78
   Long-term Strategies for Secure Relationships 81

7. NAVIGATING DIFFERENT RELATIONSHIP
   CONTEXTS   85
   Dating with Avoidant Attachment   86
   Managing Rejection Sensitivity   87
   Building Romantic Intimacy   88
   Family Relationships and Attachment Healing   89
   Creating New Family Dynamics   90
   Professional Relationships and Attachment   90

8. CONFLICT RESOLUTION AND RELATIONSHIP
   GROWTH   93
   Understanding the Root Causes of Conflict   93
   The Crucial Role of Active Listening and Empathy
   Exercises in Conflict Resolution   96
   The Importance of Setting Realistic Relationship
   Expectations   98
   Overcoming Perfectionism in Relationships   100
   Creating a Growth-Oriented Relationship Plan   102

9. INTEGRATING SELF-DISCOVERY WITH
   THERAPEUTIC SUPPORT   105
   When and Why to Seek Support   105
   Finding the Right Therapeutic Support   108
   Integrating Book Insights with Counseling   110

Developing a Therapeutic Action Plan 112
Leveraging Therapy for Long-Term Attachment
Security 114

10. FOUNDATIONS OF EMPOWERMENT AND
GROWTH IN ATTACHMENT HEALING 117
The Journey to Secure Attachment 118
Empowerment Through Knowledge and Awareness 120
Strategies for Sustainable Personal Change 121

11. TOOLS FOR TRANSFORMATION 125
Comprehensive Journaling Practice 126
Personalized Growth Planning and Goal Setting 131
Use Healthy Attachment Exercises Daily 135
Building a Supportive Community 138

12. LEGACY AND LONG-TERM GROWTH 143
Creating Your Vision for Secure Relationships 143
Breaking the Cycle of Attachment Dissatisfaction 148
Creating Your Secure Attachment Legacy 153

Conclusion 157
Appendix: Digital Communication and Avoidant
Attachment 161
Further Reading 171

INTRODUCTION

I once overheard a conversation in a bustling coffee shop that resonated deeply. A woman was candidly sharing her struggles with relationships. "I just can't seem to get close to people," she confessed with a tinge of frustration. Her words, I realized, echoed a shared experience. They mirrored the journey of many who grapple with avoidant attachment. This prevalent yet often misconstrued pattern can leave us feeling isolated, even when surrounded by those who care about us. In this shared struggle, you are not alone.

Avoidant attachment is a way of relating to others when getting too close feels overwhelming. It is like having a personal space bubble that is too big. This pattern often starts in childhood as a way to protect ourselves from getting hurt. But over the years, it can lead to feeling lonely and having relationships that do not feel quite right. Understanding this concept is the first step in turning these patterns into relationships that feel safe and loving.

My book will help you transform your life from avoidance to connection. I want to instill in you the belief that change is not just a distant dream but a tangible reality within your grasp. You can transition toward secure attachments that bring joy and fulfillment. We will explore ways to recognize dismissive patterns, identify triggers, and build secure relationships.

I am passionate about this work because I have seen the impact avoidant attachment can have. In my life, I have watched many people close to me struggle with this challenge. The distance and pain it caused were profound. These experiences fueled my desire to help others overcome similar struggles, showing me the power of transformation and the beauty of connection.

This book is structured to take you on a journey of discovery and transformation. The first chapters explore the origins and signs of avoidant attachment. We discuss how these patterns develop and how they affect our relationships. As we move forward, we delve into understanding their roots and identifying personal triggers. The latter chapters focus on practical strategies to foster secure attachments. We look at ways to build trust and intimacy and nurture healthy connections.

While the road to change can be daunting, I want to reassure you that you are not alone. I am your companion, offering practical tools and supportive guidance to help you navigate your journey. Each chapter is meticulously designed to provide insights and exercises that will support your growth and healing. As you progress, you will find that the effort you invest leads to meaningful rewards.

Self-awareness is a key element of this transformation. By engaging with the material, you will embark on a path of self-discovery. This journey encourages you to look within to understand your patterns and embrace opportunities for growth. It is about becoming more open to love, trust, and vulnerability.

I invite you to embrace this journey with an open heart and mind. The path to secure, loving relationships is within reach. Together, we can work through the challenges and celebrate the victories. Let us begin this transformative journey toward deeper connections and a more fulfilling life. The possibility of change awaits.

CHAPTER 1
UNDERSTANDING AVOIDANT ATTACHMENT

A COLLEAGUE ONCE SHARED A STORY THAT MIGHT RESONATE WITH you. After years of shallow relationships, he met someone who seemed perfect. Yet, whenever things became too intimate, he felt an overwhelming urge to pull away. It was as if an invisible force prevented him from embracing connection. This is a common experience for those with avoidant attachment—an attachment style that can deeply impact how we form and sustain meaningful relationships. However, understanding its roots is not just crucial —it is transformative. It is a beacon of hope that allows you to see the patterns that have shaped your life and the pathways to change. This chapter focuses on uncovering the origins of avoidant attachment, offering insight into why you might feel the way you do, and helping you to recognize how these patterns influence your current relationships. Let us explore this together, diving into the core theories and ideas that shed light on the development of avoidant attachment.

THE ROOTS OF AVOIDANT ATTACHMENT: CHILDHOOD WOUNDS AND EARLY EXPERIENCES

Understanding avoidant attachment begins with the pioneering work of John Bowlby and Mary Ainsworth. Bowlby, a British psychoanalyst, believed that children are biologically programmed to develop attachments as a means of survival. He proposed that these attachments form during a critical period in early childhood, typically up to five years of age. Bowlby suggested that the nature of these initial attachments creates an internal working model, a mental blueprint that guides future relationships. His theory emphasized the importance of a primary attachment figure, often a parent, whose behaviors shape the child's perception of relationships. Mary Ainsworth expanded on Bowlby's ideas through her groundbreaking "Strange Situation" experiment, which observed children's reactions to separations and reunions with their caregivers. This research identified several attachment styles, including the "avoidant style," where children showed little distress upon separation and avoided contact during reunion. These behaviors often reflect early experiences with caregivers who may have been emotionally distant or inconsistent. Ainsworth's work underscored the significance of caregiver sensitivity, suggesting that a lack of emotional responsiveness from caregivers can lead to an avoidant attachment style.

Early childhood experiences play a pivotal role in shaping avoidant attachment. Children who experience neglect or emotional unavailability from caregivers often learn to suppress their need for closeness as a self-protective measure. When a child's bids for attention are frequently ignored or met with indifference, they may begin to associate vulnerability with rejection. This can lead to the development of self-reliance, where the child learns to depend on themselves rather than risk disappointment. Inconsistent caregiving, where attention and affection are unpredictable, can further reinforce these patterns. Children in such environments often become adept at masking their emotions, shielding themselves from the pain of unmet needs. As these children grow, they may carry these patterns into adulthood, struggling with intimacy and connection in their personal relationships. The role of these early experiences in shaping avoidant attachment is profound and cannot be overstated.

The neurological underpinnings of avoidant attachment offer additional insight into how these patterns develop. Research indicates that the amygdala, a part of the brain that processes emotions and detects threats, plays a crucial role. For individuals with avoidant attachment, the amygdala may become sensitized to emotional closeness, interpreting it as a threat. This can trigger a physiological response that encourages distancing behaviors. Moreover, the brain's neuroplasticity, its ability to form new connections and pathways, suggests that attachment styles are not fixed. While early experiences set the stage, the brain retains the capacity to change and adapt throughout life, offering hope for those seeking to shift from avoidance to secure attachment.

The patterns established in childhood often manifest in adult relationships as avoidance of emotional intimacy and a strong inclination toward independence. You may find that you prioritize self-reliance, viewing emotional closeness as a potential risk. This can result in a reluctance to open up or share vulnerabilities with others—a protective mechanism learned early on. While this self-sufficiency can serve you well in certain aspects of life, it may also lead to challenges in forming deep, meaningful connections. However, recognizing these patterns is an important step toward change. By understanding the roots of avoidant attachment, you begin to see how early experiences have shaped your relationship dynamics. This awareness is the foundation for building more secure and fulfilling connections, offering hope for a more connected and inspiring future.

IDENTIFYING DISMISSIVE PATTERNS

In relationships, dismissive behaviors often go unnoticed but can cause profound disconnection. These behaviors manifest as emotional distancing tactics, where one might keep conversations superficial, avoiding topics that require vulnerability. For instance, when asked about their day, imagine someone offering only the bare minimum of detail or a partner who consistently changes the subject when conversations become too personal. This subtle withdrawal can create a chasm between people, fostering feelings of loneliness for both.

Emotional distancing is not limited to silence or brevity. It often involves the use of humor as a shield. Picture a friend who, when faced with a serious question about their feelings, responds with a joke, redirecting the conversation. This tactic can diffuse tension momentarily but leaves deeper issues unresolved. Such patterns are more than habits; they stem from a psychological need to protect oneself.

Intellectualization is another defense mechanism. It occurs when individuals focus on facts or logic to avoid confronting emotions. In a heated discussion, for example, someone might cling to data or historical references, steering clear of the emotional core of the matter. This behavior is rooted in a fear of vulnerability and dependence. By staying in the realm of the intellectual, individuals maintain control over the situation, safeguarding their emotional autonomy.

The motivations behind these dismissive patterns are often complex. Fear of vulnerability looms large, as opening up emotionally might feel like relinquishing control. For those with avoidant attachment, dependence on others can feel threatening. The desire to maintain autonomy becomes paramount, leading to behaviors that might push others away. This need for control can be traced back to early experiences, where relying on others may have led to disappointment or rejection.

Recognizing these patterns is the first step toward change. Reflective journaling could be a powerful tool in this process for some people. It allows you to explore your interactions and identify moments where you may have deflected genuine connection. Consider setting aside time each week to jot down instances where you felt the urge to distance yourself emotionally. Reflect on what triggered this reaction and how it made you feel. This self-reflection empowers you to take control of your attachment style and make positive changes. It is not just a tool but a powerful weapon in your arsenal that empowers you to take control of your attachment style and make positive changes.

Another method is seeking feedback from those around you. Feedback sessions can provide valuable insights. Ask trusted friends or close family members to share their perspectives on your communication style. How do they perceive your responses during emotionally charged conversations? This external viewpoint can illuminate blind spots you might not see on your own, providing support and understanding as you navigate your attachment style.

As you become more attuned to these dismissive tendencies, you can begin to address them. The goal is not to criticize but to understand. By acknowledging these patterns, you open the door to healthier ways of relating. Embracing vulnerability, although daunting, can lead to deeper connections and a richer emotional life. This shift requires patience and compassion for yourself and those you interact with. Remember, change is a gradual process, and each step you take brings you closer to more fulfilling relationships.

THE IMPACT ON PERSONAL RELATIONSHIPS

Avoidant attachment can cast a shadow over romantic relationships, often manifesting as emotional unavailability. When partners seek closeness, those with avoidant tendencies may retreat, creating a barrier that is difficult to overcome. This emotional distance can make expressing affection challenging. It is not uncommon to hear someone say, "I love you," only to be met with silence or a change of subject. For the partner, this can feel like rejection, fostering insecurity and doubt. Over time, these moments of withdrawal can accumulate, leading to a cycle of frustration and misunderstanding. Avoidant individuals might not even realize the extent of their emotional unavailability. They may believe they are being open, yet their actions suggest otherwise. This disconnect between intention and behavior can strain relationships, leaving both partners feeling isolated.

Friendships and family dynamics are not immune to the effects of avoidant attachment. Superficial connections often characterize friendships, where interactions remain on the surface. While discussions about the latest movies or weekend plans are common, conversations rarely venture into deeper emotional territory. This can result in friendships that lack depth and intimacy. In family settings, avoidant individuals might withdraw during conflicts, preferring silence to confrontation. This withdrawal can prevent issues from being addressed, leading to unresolved tension. Family members may perceive this as indifference or a lack of concern, further complicating relationships. Avoidant attachment can create a pattern of emotional detachment, making it difficult to form and maintain meaningful connections with those closest to us.

The cycle of relationship dissatisfaction often begins with these patterns of emotional distancing and withdrawal. Avoidant individuals struggle with emotional depth, finding it difficult to engage in the kind of vulnerable exchanges that strengthen bonds. Their partners, family members, or friends, in turn, may perceive this as neglect or emotional coldness, leading to feelings of inadequacy and loneliness. Eventually, these perceptions can erode the foundation of a relationship, leading to break-ups or persistent dissatisfaction. This cycle can repeat itself across different relationships, with each person in a relationship with the avoidant person facing the same challenges. It can feel as though no matter how hard people try, the outcome remains unchanged, leaving everyone feeling stuck and powerless.

Breaking free from these patterns requires deliberate effort and a willingness to change. Developing emotional literacy is a crucial first step if you have avoidant tendencies. This involves becoming attuned to your emotions and learning to express them more openly. It might feel uncomfortable at first, but with practice, it becomes easier. Engaging in honest and open dialogue with loved ones can also help bridge the emotional gap. This means sharing your thoughts and feelings, even when they are difficult to articulate. It is about creating a space where both parties feel heard and understood. Again, seeking feedback from trusted partners, family, or friends can provide valuable insights into how your behaviors are perceived. This external perspective can help illuminate blind spots, offering a clearer picture of how your actions impact your relationships.

Reflection Section: Strengthening Emotional Connections

Consider setting aside time weekly to reflect on your interactions. Ask yourself: *When did I feel the urge to withdraw? What emotions was I trying to avoid?* How did my actions affect my partner, family member, or friend? Jot down your thoughts in a journal, and revisit them regularly to track your progress. After several months, this practice can help you identify patterns and triggers, paving the way for change. Engaging in this reflective process allows for personal insight and growth, empowering you to take control of your relational dynamics.

AVOIDANT ATTACHMENT IN PROFESSIONAL SETTINGS

Avoidant attachment does not limit its influence to personal relationships; it often extends into professional environments, subtly shaping how we navigate the workplace. Picture a team meeting where ideas are exchanged freely. For an individual with avoidant tendencies, the thought of voicing an opinion might feel daunting. This reluctance to collaborate stems from a deep-seated preference for working independently. In a setting that thrives on teamwork, such behavior can create barriers to effective collaboration. The preference for independent tasks offers a sense of control and safety, shielding us from the uncertainties of group dynamics. This inclination can lead to missed opportunities for growth and learning that only arise through shared experiences and diverse perspectives. Opting out of collaborative projects may limit their exposure to new ideas and innovations that could enhance their skills and broaden their horizons.

The impact of avoidant attachment in the workplace does not stop at mere collaboration. It extends further into career advancement, where networking and mentorship play pivotal roles. Networking, often seen as the lifeblood of professional growth, requires engagement and openness. However, the same tendencies that lead to emotional distancing in personal relationships can surface here, resulting in a reluctance to engage in networking events or seek mentorship opportunities. This can hinder career progression, as building relationships with colleagues and industry peers is crucial for professional development. Avoidant individuals might shy away from leadership roles, finding the prospect of delegating tasks or managing others uncomfortable. This avoidance can stifle career advancement, as leadership often demands the very interpersonal skills that avoidant individuals find challenging to exercise.

Emotional intelligence is a crucial factor in overcoming these avoidant tendencies at work. It is being able to recognize, understand, and manage our emotions while also empathizing with the feelings of others. In a professional context, emotional intelligence can transform interactions, enabling individuals to navigate interpersonal relationships with empathy and insight. By honing emotional intelligence, we can begin to recognize patterns of avoidance and work toward regulating these responses. This involves becoming more attuned to personal emotions and understanding how they influence behavior in the workplace. Developing this skill can pave the way for more meaningful connections with colleagues and foster an environment where open communication thrives. Empathy, a core component of emotional intelligence, helps us see situations from others' perspectives, facilitating smoother collaborations and reducing the friction that avoidant behaviors might create.

To cultivate a more inclusive and connected work environment, practical strategies can be employed. Participating in team-building exercises offers a structured way to engage with colleagues, breaking down barriers that avoidance might erect. These activities encourage interaction in a non-threatening context, allowing us to build rapport and trust gradually. Professional coaching and mentorship can also play a transformative role. Engaging with a coach provides a safe space to review personal challenges and develop strategies to overcome them. Conversely, mentorship offers guidance and insight from someone who has traversed similar paths, providing a model for effective interpersonal engagement. These resources can empower us to get out of our comfort zones and embrace moments for growth. They ultimately lead us to a more fulfilling and successful professional life.

SELF-REFLECTION: RECOGNIZING YOUR ATTACHMENT STYLE

Understanding your attachment style is a significant step toward fostering healthier relationships. It begins with self-reflection and a willingness to look inward. One practical starting point is to engage with online attachment-style quizzes. These tools offer a structured way to assess your tendencies and provide insights into how these patterns manifest in your interactions with others. While these quizzes are not definitive, they are a useful starting point for deeper exploration. Consider them a mirror reflecting aspects of your relational self that you may not have fully acknowledged. They can illuminate patterns that have long influenced how you connect with others.

Beyond quizzes, reflective writing exercises about past relationships can be powerful tools for self-discovery. Set aside time to write about your experiences with partners, family, and friends. Think about moments where you felt particularly connected or distant. What emotions did these interactions evoke? Were there common themes or triggers that seemed to recur? By examining these narratives, you can begin to identify behaviors that align with avoidant tendencies. This process is not about judgment but understanding. It is about recognizing patterns that have shaped your relational world.

Linking these behaviors to avoidant tendencies is crucial in the path to change. Reflect on your past and present relationships. Do you notice a tendency to pull away when emotions become too intense? Are there specific situations that trigger a desire to retreat? Understanding these patterns lets you anticipate and manage them better. It also empowers you to respond differently in future interactions. By recognizing your emotional triggers and responses, you can start to shift how you engage with others, paving the way for more meaningful connections.

Personalized Attachment Style Assessment and Interpretation

The journey toward understanding your attachment style begins with more comprehensive self-assessment tools. These tools are designed to provide insight into how you relate to others, offering a window into your relational patterns. Among these tools are detailed questionnaires with scoring guides, which allow you to reflect on your behaviors and responses within relationships. These questionnaires are structured to help you identify tendencies you may not have consciously recognized before. They offer a framework for introspection, encouraging you to think about how you approach intimacy, independence, and emotional expression.

Interactive online assessments also play a pivotal role in this exploration. They provide personalized feedback that can illuminate aspects of your attachment style, offering tailored insights that resonate with your experiences. Such assessments often include scenarios that mimic real-life interactions, prompting you to consider your emotional responses in a safe, reflective space. The feedback from these assessments can serve as a catalyst for deeper self-reflection, helping you connect the dots between your current behaviors and past experiences. As you work through these tools, remember that they are not definitive. They offer guidance, but your self-awareness and personal context provide the richest understanding.

Interpreting the results of these assessments is a crucial step in your self-awareness journey. Attachment styles are typically categorized as secure, anxious, or avoidant, each with distinct characteristics and implications. A secure attachment style reflects comfort with intimacy and autonomy, while an anxious style may involve a preoccupation with relationships. On the other hand, as we have pointed out, avoidant attachment often manifests as emotional distance and a preference for self-reliance. Understanding where you fall within these categories can offer clarity on how you navigate relationships. It allows you to recognize patterns that may contribute to relational challenges and provides a starting point for change.

The insights gained from these assessments should encourage ongoing self-reflection. Consider keeping a behavioral diary to track your interactions and emotional responses every week. This practice can reveal patterns that may not be immediately apparent, offering valuable insights into how your attachment style influences your daily life. Regularly setting reminders for self-assessments can also be beneficial. These periodic check-ins provide an opportunity to observe changes and growth, helping you to stay attuned to your emotional landscape.

For those eager to delve deeper into the realm of attachment, numerous resources are available to support your exploration. Recommended books and articles on attachment theory can provide a more nuanced understanding of the dynamics at play. Engaging with these resources can enrich your knowledge and offer diverse perspectives on attachment-related experiences. Online forums and communities serve as platforms for peer support, where you can share insights and learn from others on similar paths. These communities foster a sense of belonging and offer encouragement as you navigate the complexities of attachment.

Resource List: Attachment Exploration

- **Recommend Book and Articles**: Delve into *Attached* by Amir Levine and Rachel Heller for insights into adult attachment theory, or explore scholarly articles that offer deeper academic perspectives (see our Further Reading section at the end of the book).
- **Online Communities**: Consider joining forums such as Reddit's "Attachment Theory" community, where you can engage in discussions and gain support from others on a similar path.

Engage with these resources to broaden your understanding and connect with others who share your journey.

As you embark on this path of self-reflection, it is vital to approach yourself with kindness and patience. Practicing self-compassion involves recognizing that everyone has flaws and areas for growth. Self-forgiveness is a fundamental part of this process. It allows you to acknowledge past mistakes without being defined by them. Embrace affirmations and positive self-talk as tools to foster a more compassionate inner dialogue. Remind yourself that growth is a continuous process that requires time and patience. Treat yourself with the same kindness you would offer a friend. That way, you create a nurturing space for transformation.

Setting personal growth goals is an integral part of transforming your attachment style. Begin by identifying specific areas you wish to improve. Perhaps you want to be more open in expressing your emotions or become more comfortable with vulnerability. Whatever your goals, make sure they are clear and actionable. Create a personal development plan with specific milestones to track your progress. This plan acts as a roadmap, guiding you as you work toward your goals. Celebrate small victories as you go along. Each step forward takes you that much closer to your desired relational life.

As this chapter closes, remember that self-reflection is a powerful catalyst for change. By understanding your attachment style and embracing self-compassion, you put down the groundwork for healthier and more fulfilling relationships. These insights enhance your interactions with others and deepen your connection to yourself. As you continue this process, hold onto the belief that transformation is within reach. With patience and perseverance, you can cultivate the secure and loving connections you seek.

CHAPTER 2

DEEPER UNDERSTANDING AND AWARENESS OF AVOIDANT ATTACHMENT

PICTURE YOURSELF IN A BUSTLING SOCIAL SETTING, OBSERVING someone effortlessly connecting with others while you are on the fringes of conversations. This hesitation could indicate the avoidant attachment style, which values distance over a connection. Understanding your attachment style is akin to having a map that guides you through the complex terrain of your relationships. This chapter is your guide to comprehending and being aware of your avoidant attachment, providing opportunities to delve into even more strategies regarding your attachment style.

UNDERSTANDING YOUR CORE WOUNDS

At the core of avoidant attachment lies a range of core wounds—emotional scars from early experiences that shape our self-relationships and relationships with others. These wounds often stem from pivotal moments in childhood that lead to a sense of disconnection, neglect, or emotional unavailability. Delving into these core wounds is not just crucial but profoundly empowering. They form the foundation of our attachment styles and significantly influence our adult relationships. However, understanding them gives us the power to change our responses, putting us in the driver's seat of our emotional journey.

Core wounds often manifest in feelings of inadequacy, fear of intimacy, and a pervasive sense of unworthiness. For individuals with avoidant attachment, these feelings can lead to the development of protective mechanisms designed to shield them from emotional pain. These protective mechanisms could include distancing behaviors such as avoiding deep conversations, withdrawing emotionally during conflicts, finding excuses to avoid social gatherings, or even overworking to avoid emotional situations. Recognizing these wounds is the first important step toward healing and transformation.

Understanding your core wounds involves a journey of self-reflection and awareness. It may require revisiting past experiences to identify how they have influenced your beliefs about relationships and intimacy. Ask yourself: *What were the critical moments in my childhood that shaped my views on love and connection? How have these experiences manifested in my current relationships?*

As we touched on in the previous chapter, a common theme among many individuals with avoidant attachment is a history of unreliable or emotionally distant caregivers. This often leads to internal narratives that promote self-sufficiency at the cost of intimacy. Recognizing and acknowledging these narratives is essential for breaking the cycle of avoidance. By doing so, you can begin to challenge and reframe the negative beliefs that have held you back.

Additionally, exploring your core wounds helps illuminate your triggers—those situations or interactions that provoke a defensive response. Understanding what triggers your avoidant behaviors can empower you to respond more consciously rather than reactively. For example, feelings of being overwhelmed or vulnerable may prompt you to withdraw. By acknowledging these triggers, you can work toward developing healthier coping mechanisms and fostering a deeper sense of connection with others.

Ultimately, the process of understanding your core wounds is not about assigning blame but rather about fostering compassion for yourself. As you learn to acknowledge and process these wounds, you create space for healing and the possibility of establishing secure connections. By transforming avoidance into awareness, you open the door to genuine intimacy and emotional resilience, allowing for nurturing relationships that celebrate your authentic self.

IDENTIFYING EMOTIONAL TRIGGERS

Emotional triggers are like hidden landmines in the landscape of our relationships, waiting to be activated by specific situations or interactions. When triggered, they often lead to intense emotional responses, disrupting harmony and understanding. These triggers usually stem from past experiences, are deeply ingrained in our psyche, and affect how we perceive and react in the present. However, understanding these triggers can bring a profound sense of relief, as it lets us recognize when our reactions are more about old wounds than the current situation, easing the tension in our relationships and providing a sense of calm and control.

Identifying your emotional triggers requires thoughtful introspection and a willingness to engage in self-inquiry. Start by reflecting on recent interactions that elicited strong emotional reactions. Ask yourself, *What about that moment made me feel uncomfortable or defensive?* Again, consider keeping a journal where you document these instances. Write down the situation, your feelings, and any physical sensations you experienced. As weeks pass, patterns may emerge, revealing specific themes or scenarios that consistently trigger your avoidant behaviors. Once again, this reflective practice can be complemented by getting feedback from trusted friends or family members. Sometimes, others can see patterns in our behavior that we might miss. Open a dialogue with someone you trust and ask for their observations on how you react in certain situations. These talks can provide valuable insights into your emotional landscape.

The origins of these emotional triggers often lie in our past, shaped by childhood experiences or previous relationships. If, as a child, you learned that expressing needs led to disappointment or rejection, you might have developed a trigger around vulnerability. Similarly, a history of relationships where trust was broken can lead to triggers related to intimacy or dependence. By linking these past experiences to your current emotional responses, you have a deeper understanding of why certain situations provoke strong reactions. This awareness can empower you to separate the past from the present and approach situations with greater clarity and calm.

Developing strategies to manage these triggers is an essential step in mitigating their impact. But it is not just about mitigation. It is about control. One effective approach is to cultivate coping mechanisms that help you remain grounded when faced with a trigger. Mindfulness methods like guided meditation, deep breathing, or a short walk can be particularly beneficial. These practices encourage you to stay present and observe your emotions without judgment, allowing you to respond thoughtfully rather than react impulsively. Engaging in mindfulness regularly can enhance your emotional regulation skills, making it easier to navigate challenging interactions. Other coping mechanisms could include journaling, talking to a trusted friend, or engaging in a physical activity. This sense of control can build your confidence, making it easier to implement these strategies when triggers arise.

BUILDING EMOTIONAL SELF-AWARENESS

Emotional self-awareness is recognizing and understanding your feelings and how they affect your thinking and behaviors. It is a cornerstone of personal growth and healthy relationships. When emotionally self-aware, you can navigate social interactions with greater ease and empathy. This awareness allows you to identify and articulate your feelings, reducing misunderstandings and enhancing communication. It also connects closely with emotional intelligence, which involves recognizing your emotions and those of others. By honing emotional self-awareness, you are better equipped to respond to emotional challenges with resilience and clarity, improving your mental health and relational interactions. The benefits extend beyond personal insight; they foster a deeper connection with those around you, leading to more meaningful and supportive relationships and a profound sense of emotional preparedness.

Engaging in practical exercises can be very beneficial in cultivating this self-awareness. One method is mood tracking, which can be done using apps or a simple journal. By noting your emotions at different times of the day, you begin to see patterns in your emotional responses. This practice helps identify triggers and understand the context in which certain emotions arise. For instance, you might notice a surge of anxiety every Monday morning, prompting you to explore what about that time triggers such a response. Another exercise is a daily reflection on emotional experiences. Set aside a few minutes each day to think about the emotions you felt and what prompted them. Write down these reflections, focusing on how these emotions influenced your actions and decisions. Over a while, these practices can illuminate your emotional landscape, offering insights into how your feelings shape your interactions.

Mindfulness plays a vital role in improving emotional self-awareness. It involves paying attention to the present moment without judgment, allowing you to observe your emotions as they arise. Through mindfulness practices, such as breathing exercises, you can stay grounded when emotions intensify. These exercises help you remain present, reducing the tendency to react impulsively. For example, when you feel anger building, taking slow, deep breaths can help you pause and consider your response. Guided meditations focusing on emotional exploration further deepen this practice. They prompt you to explore emotions with curiosity, encouraging a non-reactive stance. Such meditations guide you through acknowledging emotions, understanding their origin, and letting them pass without clinging to them. Regular mindfulness cultivates awareness that permeates your daily life, fostering a calmer, more measured approach to emotional challenges.

The journey of emotional self-awareness is ongoing and requires a commitment to continuous exploration. Creating a personalized emotional development plan can guide this process. Start by setting specific goals for your emotional growth, such as developing greater patience or reducing anxiety in social settings. Write down steps to achieve these goals, incorporating practices like journaling or mindfulness into your routine. Regularly review and adjust your plan as you gain insights and progress. Additionally, dedicate time for introspection, whether it is through meditation, quiet reflection, or engaging with nature. This time allows you to connect with your inner self, assess your emotional state, and recalibrate your approach to challenges. By prioritizing emotional self-awareness, you empower yourself to navigate the complexities of relationships and life with greater understanding and empathy.

UNDERSTANDING AVOIDANT BEHAVIORS IN CONFLICT

Imagine you are in a disagreement with a partner. The conversation escalates, and suddenly, there is a wall. You find yourself emotionally checked out, hearing words but not processing them. This is a classic avoidant conflict behavior— stonewalling or withdrawing entirely when things get heated. It is a protective mechanism, a way to avoid the discomfort that comes with confrontation. For many with avoidant attachment, facing conflict feels like standing on shaky ground. The thought of exposing vulnerabilities or emotions can be overwhelming, leading to a retreat into silence. This withdrawal might seem like a safe haven, but it often leaves issues unresolved, allowing resentment to fester. Over the years, these unaddressed conflicts can pile up, creating a rift in the relationship. Trust erodes, and emotional intimacy fades as partners feel shut out and unimportant.

The motivations behind the avoidance of conflicts are deeply rooted. At its core is a fear of vulnerability. Opening up in the heat of an argument might feel like an invitation to be hurt. There is a desire to maintain control and manage emotions and situations. This control protects against the chaos of emotional exposure. But it can also mean that significant issues remain unspoken, festering beneath the surface. You might find that conflicts are avoided not because they are unimportant but because the emotional stakes feel too high. This avoidance creates a cycle where conflicts are not resolved but delayed, leading to more significant issues down the line.

The impact of these avoidant behaviors on relationships can be profound. When partners, family members, or friends consistently face a wall of silence or emotional absence, they may begin to question the strength and validity of the relationship. Trust, the foundation of every healthy relationship, can start to crumble. Without open communication, misunderstandings thrive, and others may feel increasingly isolated. The lack of resolution leaves wounds open, which can deepen as time passes, eroding the connection that once existed. Emotional intimacy, the closeness from sharing and understanding each other's inner worlds, becomes more challenging. As each conflict ends without resolution, the space between you and your significant others grows, filled with unspoken words and unmet needs.

To approach conflict in a healthier, more constructive manner, it is crucial to embrace new strategies. Assertive communication is a powerful tool in this transformation. It involves expressing your thoughts and needs clearly and respectfully, without aggression or passivity. Start by using "I" statements, focusing on your feelings rather than placing blame. For example, instead of saying, "You never listen to me," try, "I feel unheard when we don't discuss things." This shift in language can open dialogue and reduce defensiveness. Active listening complements assertive communication by ensuring both people feel heard. It requires you to engage fully, reflecting back what you hear to confirm understanding. This practice fosters empathy, allowing you to see the situation from the other person's perspective. By acknowledging their feelings, you build a bridge of understanding, making it easier to find common ground.

Empathy plays a crucial role during disagreements. It helps you step outside your experience and consider how others might feel. Practicing empathy involves asking questions and genuinely listening to the answers, even when they might be difficult to hear. It is about creating a safe space for both people to discuss their thoughts and feelings without fear of judgment. When empathy is present, conflicts transform from battles to collaborative problem-solving opportunities. Both people can work together to find solutions that honor each other's needs and perspectives. This approach resolves the immediate issue and strengthens the relationship, building trust and deepening emotional intimacy. By incorporating these strategies, you pave the way for healthier interactions, creating a foundation for a more connected and resilient relationship. We will explore strategies for conflict resolution in more depth in Chapter 8.

OVERCOMING FEAR OF INTIMACY

Intimacy is a multifaceted concept, pivotal for meaningful relationships. It goes beyond physical closeness, encompassing emotional intimacy, which involves sharing our innermost thoughts and feelings. This level of openness deepens connections, fostering a bond that withstands life's challenges. Emotional intimacy allows you to be seen and understood, creating a foundation of trust and vulnerability. It is the glue that holds relationships together, providing a space where people feel safe to express their true selves. Without it, relationships can feel superficial, lacking the depth that brings fulfillment and joy. Yet, many find themselves hesitating at the threshold of intimacy, unsure of how to step forward without fear.

Avoidant individuals often grapple with a fear of intimacy, a barrier rooted in past experiences. Memories of betrayal or rejection can linger, casting a shadow over present relationships. These experiences can instill a belief that vulnerability equates to risk, leading to a protective instinct to keep others at a distance. Internal beliefs about self-worth also play a role, as those who doubt their value may fear that true intimacy will expose their perceived inadequacies. This fear can manifest as reluctance to engage emotionally, keeping relationships at arm's length to avoid potential pain. The result is often a cycle of loneliness and isolation, where the desire for connection is overshadowed by the fear of being hurt or rejected.

To embrace intimacy, starting small can make the journey less daunting. Begin with small acts of vulnerability, like sharing a personal story or admitting a fear. These moments of openness, though seemingly minor, can pave the way for a deeper connection. They build a bridge of trust, demonstrating to you and your partner, family member, or friend that vulnerability does not always lead to harm. Consistent, open communication also plays a vital role. Regularly discussing thoughts and feelings with others fosters an environment where intimacy can thrive. It encourages honesty and transparency and fosters a safe space for both people to express themselves without fear of judgment. After a few months, these practices can begin dismantling the walls that fear has built, allowing intimacy to flourish.

Building trust with oneself is equally vital in overcoming the fear of intimacy. Trusting yourself involves believing in your resilience and ability to handle emotional exposure. Exercises in self-trust and self-compassion can support this process. Practice affirmations that reinforce your worth and remind you that you are capable and deserve love. Engaging in activities that nurture your self-esteem, such as pursuing hobbies or setting personal goals, can also strengthen this trust. As you cultivate self-trust, your capacity to trust others naturally expands, creating a foundation for deeper connections.

Strengthening trust in relationships is crucial for fostering intimacy. Shared experiences, like traveling together or embarking on a new project, can build a sense of teamwork and mutual support. These experiences create memories and bonds that deepen over the years. They also provide opportunities to practice vulnerability in a supportive environment. By navigating challenges together, you learn to rely on each other, reinforcing the trust that intimacy requires. This process takes time and patience, but each step brings you closer to the fulfilling relationships you desire. We will explore ways to deepen trust and intimacy even further in Chapters 5 and 6.

UNDERSTANDING SHAME AND SELF-WORTH

The relationship between shame and avoidant attachment runs deep, often beginning in our earliest experiences of disconnection and perceived unworthiness. When young children experience consistent emotional unavailability or criticism from caregivers, they associate their needs and feelings with a sense of being fundamentally flawed. This creates what we call the shame-withdrawal cycle, where the experience of shame triggers emotional withdrawal, which then reinforces feelings of isolation and unworthiness.

Consider Tammy's story of growing up, with her academic achievements celebrated while her emotional needs were often dismissed with phrases like "Don't be so sensitive" or "You're too needy." As an adult, Tammy found herself unable to ask for support at work or in relationships, experiencing intense shame whenever she felt vulnerable. Her pattern of withdrawal, while protective in childhood, now prevented her from forming the deep connections she desired.

Understanding shame requires distinguishing between healthy shame—which serves as a moral compass and helps us maintain social bonds—and toxic shame, which convinces us we are inherently defective. For those with avoidant attachment, toxic shame often manifests as perfectionism, emotional distance, and an intense fear of being "seen." This shame becomes a lens through which all relationships are viewed, creating a self-fulfilling prophecy of disconnection.

Building Self-Worth Beyond Achievement

Building authentic self-worth begins with recognizing how deeply our sense of value has been tied to external validation and achievement. Many individuals with avoidant attachment develop what psychologists call a "false self"—a carefully constructed persona based on accomplishments, competence, and self-sufficiency. While this strategy may bring professional success, it often leaves a profound inner emptiness.

Take Wendell's experience as a successful entrepreneur. He appeared to have everything —wealth, status, and peer admiration. Yet in therapy, Wendell revealed that he felt like an impostor, constantly afraid that others would discover he was not truly worthy of connection. His worth was so entangled with his achievements that any failure felt catastrophic, leading him to avoid close relationships where he might be judged imperfect.

The process of developing internal validation requires a fundamental shift in self-relationship. This involves learning to recognize and honor our inherent worth separate from our accomplishments. Through consistent self-reflection and compassionate self-dialogue, we challenge the deeply held belief that we must earn love through performance or self-sufficiency.

Breaking the Shame Cycle

Disrupting entrenched shame patterns requires both awareness and active intervention. The first step is learning to recognize shame reactions in their earliest stages. These often begin with subtle physical sensations—a tightening in the chest, a desire to disappear, or a sudden sense of exposure. By developing this awareness, we can respond differently to shame triggers rather than automatically withdrawing.

Ellen's journey illustrates this transformation. As a teacher, she initially responded to any classroom challenges by becoming rigid and withdrawn, her shame about potential imperfection preventing her from connecting with students or seeking colleague support. Through therapy, Ellen learned to recognize her shame response as it emerged. She developed a practice of taking three deep breaths when feeling triggered and reminding herself that vulnerability is not weakness but rather a pathway to authentic connection.

The development of shame resilience involves creating new neural pathways through repeated experiences of safe vulnerability. This might begin in therapy, where the consistent presence of an attuned therapist helps reconstruct our expectations of a relationship. As we experience acceptance in moments of vulnerability, our nervous system gradually learns that connection, rather than withdrawal, can be a source of safety.

SOMATIC AWARENESS AND HEALING

Our bodies hold the imprint of our attachment histories, often expressing through tension patterns what we cannot yet verbalize. Understanding the somatic dimension of avoidant attachment opens new healing pathways beyond cognitive insight. When properly attended to, the body's wisdom can guide us toward greater security and connection.

The case of James exemplifies the importance of body-based awareness. Despite years of talk therapy, James struggled to understand why he consistently withdrew from potential romantic partners. Through somatic work, he discovered that he habitually held his breath and tensed his shoulders when others expressed care for him. This physical pattern, developed in childhood to protect against disappointment, actively maintained his avoidance in adult relationships.

Somatic Exercises for Regulation

Through intentional somatic practices, the body's wisdom in healing attachment wounds becomes accessible. These exercises bridge our conscious awareness with the deeper, often unconscious, patterns that maintain avoidant attachment. Through regular practice, we can begin to reshape our nervous system's default responses to connection and intimacy.

Dr. Rachel Chen, a trauma-informed therapist, shares her client, Michael's transformation. Initially, Michael could only identify his attachment activation through hindsight after withdrawing from connections. Through guided somatic work, he learned to recognize the subtle tightening in his throat that preceded emotional shutdown. This awareness became his early warning system, allowing him to pause and implement regulation strategies before withdrawal.

Breathwork is a fundamental tool in attachment healing, as our breathing patterns directly influence our nervous system. "box breathing"—inhaling for four counts, holding for four, exhaling for four, and holding for four—helps activate the parasympathetic nervous system, creating a physiological state more conducive to connection. When practiced regularly, these breathing patterns can become automatic responses to attachment stress, replacing old withdrawal patterns.

As we conclude this chapter, consider how these insights into intimacy, trust, and self-worth can transform relationships. You can build more profound, more meaningful connections by embracing vulnerability, nurturing self-trust, fostering open communication, and breaking the shame cycle. These steps set the stage for creating secure attachments, the focus of our next exploration.

CHAPTER 3
CULTURAL AND GLOBAL CONTEXTS OF ATTACHMENT

IMAGINE STANDING IN A VIBRANT MARKET, ALIVE WITH COLORS, sounds, and scents worldwide. Each stall represents a different culture, offering unique flavors and traditions. Just as these stalls add richness to the marketplace, cultural norms and values are pivotal in shaping our understanding of relationships and attachment. These norms significantly influence how we express our emotions and perceive independence, impacting our attachment styles.

Understanding attachment patterns must be viewed through cultural diversity and modern social contexts. What might be interpreted as avoidant behavior in one culture could represent healthy boundaries in another. This complexity becomes particularly evident in our increasingly interconnected world, where relationships often span cultural boundaries.

Consider the experience of Mei, a first-generation Chinese American therapist working with predominantly Western clients. She observed how her cultural background, which valued emotional restraint and indirect communication, initially led to her being labeled as avoidant by Western colleagues. Through a deeper exploration of cultural attachment variations, she began to understand how cultural values shape the expression of attachment needs and the pathways to security.

Religious and spiritual traditions also significantly influence attachment patterns and healing approaches. For instance, in some Buddhist communities, the practice of non-attachment is highly valued, potentially creating confusion around Western attachment theory's emphasis on secure dependency. Understanding these cultural and spiritual nuances helps create more inclusive and practical approaches to attachment healing. This chapter will explore how these cultural influences shape avoidant attachment and affect our relationships across different societies.

UNDERSTANDING CULTURAL ATTACHMENT VARIATIONS

Cultural norms significantly influence attachment styles, with a clear distinction between collectivist and individualist societies. For instance, in collectivist cultures like those found in many Asian and African countries, the norm of prioritizing community, family, and interdependence can lead to avoidant attachment when individuals suppress personal needs to maintain harmony. In contrast, individualist cultures, prevalent in Western countries, value independence, self-reliance, and personal achievement. This focus can lead to avoidant attachments as individuals learn to prioritize autonomy over emotional connection. The societal expectation of self-sufficiency can create a barrier to forming close relationships, as emotional expression may be viewed as a sign of weakness or dependency.

Cultural upbringing is crucial in shaping attachment behaviors, with parenting styles varying across cultures. Authoritarian parenting, defined by strict demands and limited responsiveness, is prevalent in many cultures and can contribute to avoidant attachment. In these settings, children may learn to suppress their emotions and need to meet parental expectations, leading to a detachment from their emotional experiences. The ongoing influence of cultural expectations is evident in how these children navigate their relationships in adulthood. Conversely, cultures emphasizing emotional expression and nurturing caregiving often foster secure attachments. The role of extended family in attachment formation also varies culturally. In many collectivist cultures, extended family members play an integral role in a child's upbringing, providing additional sources of attachment. This can reinforce secure attachments through consistent caregiving or contribute to an avoidant attachment if family dynamics are complex or unpredictable.

Perceptions of avoidant behaviors differ across cultures, reflecting varying attitudes toward emotional expression and vulnerability. In some cultures, emotional stoicism is perceived as a strength, embodying resilience and self-control. This perspective can lead individuals to view avoidant behaviors positively as a way to maintain composure and avoid emotional entanglements. In contrast, other cultures may value vulnerability and interdependence, viewing emotional openness as a path to deeper connections. These cultural attitudes influence how individuals perceive and express their attachment styles, shaping their relational dynamics and emotional experiences.

Avoidant behaviors manifest uniquely in different cultural contexts, influenced by societal norms and expectations. In high-context cultures, where communication relies heavily on implicit understanding and nonverbal cues, individuals may avoid conflict to preserve harmony and relationships. This means that in these cultures, people often communicate in ways that are more indirect and rely on shared cultural knowledge. This avoidance can lead to unspoken tensions and unresolved issues, as confrontation is usually discouraged. Conversely, in low-context cultures, where communication is explicit and direct, individuals may prioritize privacy and personal space, leading to avoidant behaviors emphasizing autonomy over connection. People tend to communicate more directly in these cultures and rely less on shared cultural knowledge. These cultural preferences shape how individuals navigate their relationships, influencing the development and expression of avoidant attachment.

Interactive Element: Reflection Exercise on Cultural Influences

Take a moment to reflect on your cultural background and how it might have shaped your attachment style. Consider the following questions:

- How do cultural norms in your upbringing influence your view on emotional expression and independence?
- In what ways do you see cultural expectations affecting your attachment behaviors today?

- How might understanding these cultural influences empower you to navigate your relationships consciously?

Use these reflections to explore the cultural context of your attachment style, deepening your understanding of how cultural norms shape your relational experiences. This awareness can offer new insights into your behaviors, helping you bridge cultural divides and foster more meaningful connections.

EMBRACING DIVERSITY IN ATTACHMENT STYLES

Attachment styles do not exist in a vacuum in the rich tapestry of human relationships. They weave through the cultural and social fabric surrounding them, each representing a unique blend of influences. Recognizing the diversity within attachment styles is crucial, as it highlights how cultural contexts shape our emotional connections. In culturally diverse societies, attachment styles are not homogeneous. Secure, anxious, and avoidant styles adapt and manifest differently, colored by the cultural nuances that define them. This recognition of diversity within attachment styles opens our minds to the unique and intricate nature of human relationships, allowing us to see beyond a one-size-fits-all approach and appreciate the richness of different perspectives.

Exploring the benefits of diverse attachment perspectives enriches our understanding and broadens our relational horizons. For example, collectivist cultures often emphasize the importance of community and support, teaching us valuable lessons about the strength and resilience found in interdependence. These cultures show how collective support systems can create a safety net that fosters secure attachment. They provide individuals with the confidence to explore and express their emotions. On the other hand, individualistic cultures highlight the value of independence and self-reliance, reminding us of the importance of personal autonomy within relationships. This perspective, which encourages the development of personal boundaries and self-awareness, is essential for healthy attachment. By learning from these diverse approaches, we gain a deeper appreciation for how attachment can be expressed and nurtured, recognizing that each perspective offers unique insights into the human experience. This broadened understanding can enrich our relationships and interactions with others.

Embracing openness to multiple attachment narratives invites us to value the diversity of experiences and stories that shape our emotional worlds. Sharing multicultural stories and personal experiences allows us to see the world through different lenses, offering new perspectives on attachment. These narratives reveal the varied pathways to emotional connection, highlighting how people navigate and understand their relationships. Whether it is the story of a family that values interdependence or an individual who finds strength in solitude, each narrative contributes to a richer understanding of attachment. By valuing these diverse pathways, we celebrate the individuality and creativity of forming connections, acknowledging that there is no one right way to love and relate to others.

From a clinical view, therapists and counselors should adopt practical strategies that honor cultural differences to ensure that attachment work is inclusive and respects diversity. Culturally sensitive communication techniques are vital, as they help therapists and clients navigate conversations with empathy and respect. This involves being mindful of cultural norms and values and adjusting our communication style to accommodate different perspectives. Encouraging culturally informed therapeutic practices can further enhance inclusivity in attachment work. Therapists and counselors should incorporate cultural insights into their practice, acknowledging the unique cultural influences that shape their clients' attachment styles. This approach fosters a supportive environment where people feel seen and understood, empowering them to explore and transform their attachment patterns authentically. Cultivating these inclusive practices creates spaces where all individuals can meaningfully engage with attachment work, regardless of their cultural background.

Case Study: Cultural Adaptation in Therapy

Consider the story of Mei, a young woman from a collectivist culture who sought therapy in a Western context. Her therapist recognized the importance of family in Mei's life, incorporating family-oriented strategies into the sessions. By integrating Mei's cultural values into the therapeutic process, the therapist created a space where Mei felt comfortable exploring her attachment style. This culturally informed approach respected Mei's background and empowered her to navigate her relationships authentically and confidently. Mei's story illustrates the power of embracing diversity in attachment work, highlighting the transformative potential of culturally sensitive practices. (We will explore the importance of therapeutic fit in more depth in Chapter 9.)

CROSS-CULTURAL RELATIONSHIP DYNAMICS

Imagine two people from different corners of the world, each carrying their traditions and customs, coming together to build a life. Cultural backgrounds intricately shape relationship dynamics, influencing how partners interact, communicate, and set expectations. In some cultures, relationship roles and responsibilities are clearly defined, often influenced by traditions passed down through generations. For instance, in many societies, there may be an expectation for one partner to take on specific household duties or financial responsibilities. These roles can be deeply ingrained, reflecting cultural values and norms that dictate how partners should contribute to the relationship.

Additionally, cultural traditions such as courtship, marriage, and family planning can significantly impact relationship milestones. What might be considered a romantic gesture in one culture could be seen as inappropriate in another, highlighting the importance of understanding and respecting these differences. When individuals from diverse backgrounds come together, navigating these variations requires openness and adaptability, as each partner brings their cultural expectations to the relationship.

Cross-cultural relationships often face unique challenges that require careful navigation. Differing family expectations can pose significant hurdles, as families may hold traditional views that clash. For example, one partner's family might expect a formal engagement and marriage ceremony, while the other might prioritize personal choice over tradition. Balancing these expectations can be daunting, requiring clear communication and compromise to honor both cultures. Language and communication barriers also present challenges, as linguistic differences can lead to misinterpretations and misunderstandings. Even when partners share a common language, cultural nuances can affect how messages are conveyed and received. Miscommunication can strain relationships, making developing effective strategies to bridge these gaps crucial. Partners must learn to communicate with patience and empathy, recognizing that cultural differences can influence how each person expresses emotions and intentions.

Despite these challenges, cross-cultural relationships offer unique strengths and opportunities for growth. The blending of diverse perspectives can lead to innovative solutions and enriched experiences. Each partner brings their own worldview, which is shaped by their cultural background, which can broaden their understanding and appreciation of different ways of life. This diversity fosters creativity and adaptability as partners learn to navigate and embrace their differences. Additionally, navigating cultural differences builds resilience. It strengthens the relationship as partners work together to overcome obstacles. These experiences can deepen the emotional bond, fostering a sense of unity and collaboration. Cross-cultural relationships encourage personal growth as individuals gain insight into their cultural identities and develop a greater appreciation for the richness of diversity.

Practical tools can be employed to enhance understanding and harmony in cross-cultural relationships. Engaging in cultural exchange activities and experiences can provide valuable insights into each other's backgrounds and traditions. Participating in cultural events, cooking traditional meals together, or learning each other's languages can foster appreciation and respect for each culture's uniqueness. These activities create opportunities for shared discovery, allowing partners or friends to connect more deeply. Creating a shared cultural space within the relationship can also strengthen the bond. This involves integrating elements from both cultures into daily life, such as celebrating holidays from each partner's background or establishing new traditions that honor both heritages. By blending cultural influences, partners create a unique cultural identity that reflects their shared journey. These practices promote inclusion and understanding, building a strong foundation for a successful relationship.

RESPECTING CULTURAL VARIATIONS IN ATTACHMENT

Respecting cultural differences in attachment is pivotal in fostering understanding and empathy. We must look beyond our cultural lenses and appreciate how attachment manifests globally. Avoiding ethnocentric judgments is crucial. It is important not to view our cultural practices as the standard by which others are measured. Instead, embracing cultural humility allows us to explore attachment with an open heart and mind. Cultural humility involves recognizing that our understanding is limited and that there is always more to learn from others' experiences and perspectives. This mindset fosters respect for how people connect and form attachments, acknowledging that no single way is superior.

Cultural awareness has a significant role in building stronger, more empathetic relationships. By understanding the cultural context in which our partners operate, we can better appreciate their perspectives and responses. This awareness allows us to navigate interactions with sensitivity and awareness, recognizing how cultural values and norms influence behaviors and expectations. Incorporating cultural knowledge into relationship decisions enables us to make choices that honor both peoples' backgrounds, fostering harmony and mutual respect. For instance, considering each partner's cultural traditions and values can strengthen the relationship when planning significant life events or discussing future goals. This approach enhances communication and deepens the emotional connection, as both people feel seen and valued.

Culturally respectful communication is key to ensuring that interactions are inclusive and considerate of cultural differences. Adapting communication styles to align with cultural norms helps facilitate understanding and reduce potential conflicts. For example, straightforward and clear communication can prevent misunderstandings in cultures where direct communication is valued; conversely, in coordinating indirect communication, being sensitive to nonverbal cues and using subtle language may be more effective. Practicing active cultural listening—attuning oneself to the cultural nuances in conversations—and empathy enhances our ability to engage in meaningful dialogue. It involves being present, asking open-ended questions, and showing genuine interest in understanding the other person's perspective. This practice can bridge cultural divides, fostering a sense of connection and trust.

Learning from diverse cultural practices enriches our relationships and broadens our perspectives. Celebrating multicultural traditions and customs allows us to embrace the richness of different cultures and incorporate their wisdom into our lives. Participating in cultural festivals, ceremonies, or family gatherings gives us insight into the values and beliefs that shape different communities. Incorporating multicultural rituals into our relationship life can also deepen our connection to our partners and their backgrounds. Whether adopting a traditional practice or creating new rituals that honor both cultures, these experiences foster a sense of belonging and unity. They remind us of the beauty of diversity and the myriad ways we can express love and connection.

Imagine a couple integrating each other's cultural customs into their daily routine. They might start their mornings with a traditional breakfast from one partner's culture and end their evenings with a bedtime ritual from the other. This blending of traditions creates a unique cultural tapestry that reflects their shared journey. It also is a constant reminder of their commitment to understanding and valuing each other's heritage. By embracing these diverse practices, they enrich their relationship and strengthen their appreciation for the cultural influences that have shaped them.

Respecting cultural variations in attachment opens the possibility of more profound, meaningful connections. Valuing the diverse ways people form attachments cultivates empathy and understanding, creating a world where all forms of connection are honored and celebrated. This approach enriches our relationships and contributes to a more inclusive and harmonious global community.

INCLUSIVE STRATEGIES FOR A GLOBAL COMMUNITY

As we consider the needs of a global village, it is vital to acknowledge the diverse backgrounds, experiences, and perspectives we all bring to the table. People from different parts of the world may approach attachment with various cultural lenses, which shape their understanding and interactions. Acknowledging these differences enriches our discussions about attachment, allowing us to tailor strategies that truly resonate. By considering global perspectives, we create an inclusive dialogue that embraces the unique experiences of individuals from all walks of life. This approach ensures that the strategies presented are culturally relevant and respectful of the diversity that defines our global community.

Offering inclusive strategies for attachment improvement requires flexibility and adaptability. I am all about providing tools that can be molded to fit different cultural contexts, recognizing that one size does not fit all. Flexible attachment exercises are key, as they allow individuals to engage with the material in a way that aligns with their cultural values and norms. Encouraging readers to adapt techniques to their cultural context empowers them to take ownership of their attachment journey, fostering a sense of agency and confidence. This adaptability ensures the strategies are practical and meaningful, resonating with the individual's unique cultural identity and experiences.

Technology also plays a crucial role in bridging cultural gaps and supporting attachment work on a global scale. It offers a platform where individuals from different backgrounds can come together, share insights, and learn from each other. Online communities provide a space for cross-cultural attachment support, where people can connect with others who share similar experiences and challenges. These communities foster a sense of belonging and offer a supportive network that transcends geographical boundaries. Additionally, virtual resources for culturally informed attachment education provide access to diverse perspectives and knowledge. These resources empower individuals to explore attachment in a way that respects and honors their cultural heritage, enhancing their understanding and growth. However, we must be mindful of setting healthy expectations and boundaries around digital communication (more about this in the Appendix).

Promoting global empathy and connection is central to fostering a world where attachment work is inclusive and impactful. Engaging in international conversations about attachment encourages exchanging ideas and experiences, broadening our understanding of how attachment manifests across cultures. This dialogue fosters empathy as we learn to appreciate the unique challenges and triumphs individuals from different backgrounds face. Building international networks of attachment support and learning further strengthens this connection, creating a web of support that spans the globe. These networks offer collaboration, learning, and growth opportunities, enriching our collective understanding of attachment and its role in our lives.

In the grand tapestry of human connection, each thread represents a unique cultural perspective, weaving together a rich and diverse narrative. By embracing these perspectives, we create a world where attachment work is inclusive and transformative, empowering individuals to build meaningful, authentic, and resilient connections. As we move forward, we explore the intricate interplay of culture and attachment, recognizing the beauty and complexity that define our shared humanity. This journey is one of discovery and growth, fueled by a commitment to understanding and honoring the varied ways we connect and relate to one another.

CHAPTER 4
BRIDGING AWARENESS
AND CHANGE

THE JOURNEY FROM AWARENESS TO ACTIVE CHANGE REPRESENTS A crucial transition in addressing avoidant attachment patterns. This bridge period requires careful attention to both internal readiness for change and external support systems that will facilitate transformation.

Consider the experience of Dr. Emily Chen, who documented her transition from understanding to action in her work with attachment patterns. She describes this period as "standing in the doorway between knowing and becoming," emphasizing the importance of honoring the past protective function of avoidant patterns and the possibility of more secure attachment. She created a roadmap for others navigating this crucial transition through journals and recorded self-reflections.

Preparing for change involves creating what attachment theorists call a "secure base for exploration." This means establishing reliable support systems and self-care practices that can sustain us through the vulnerability of transformation. These foundations include therapeutic relationships, supportive friendships, somatic practices, and clear protocols for managing attachment activation during the change process.

IMPLEMENTING SUSTAINABLE CHANGE

The transition from theoretical understanding to practical change requires a carefully structured approach that honors our desire for growth and our nervous system's need for safety. This implementation phase often represents the most challenging aspect of attachment work, as it requires us to act in ways that initially feel counterintuitive or threaten our emotional safety.

The experience of Dr. Nathan Rivera, a clinical psychologist who documented his attachment journey, provides valuable insights into this implementation process. Despite his professional understanding of attachment theory, Nathan struggled to maintain connection during periods of stress. He developed the "micro-steps approach," focusing on implementing tiny, manageable changes in his daily interactions. For instance, he began by simply noticing his impulse to withdraw without changing his behavior. Over time, he progressed to pausing for five seconds before withdrawing, then gradually extending this pause while developing alternative responses.

Creating sustainable change requires understanding the difference between behavioral modification and genuine transformation. A software engineer, Amy, initially approached her attachment work as though debugging code, looking for problematic behaviors to eliminate. Through work with her therapist, she understood that sustainable change required a more profound reorganization of her emotional operating system. This meant changing specific behaviors and developing new ways of experiencing and responding to emotional connections.

MANAGING RESISTANCE AND SETBACKS

Resistance to change often emerges subtly, particularly for those with avoidant attachment patterns who have developed sophisticated strategies for maintaining emotional distance. Understanding resistance as a protective response rather than a failure allows us to work with it productively rather than against it.

Professor Marcus Chen's longitudinal study of attachment change provides valuable insights into the nature of setbacks in this work. His research followed fifty individuals through their attachment transformation journey, documenting what he termed "recursive growth patterns"—where apparent setbacks served as opportunities for deeper integration of new patterns. One participant, Linda, described how a period of intense withdrawal following a vulnerable emotional exchange initially felt like a failure but ultimately led to a deeper understanding of her attachment needs and triggers.

The development of resilience during setbacks involves creating what attachment theorist Mary Main called "earned security." This process requires building internal resources that allow us to maintain a connection to our growth process, even during periods of activation or withdrawal. These resources include self-compassion practices, clear protocols for re-engagement after withdrawal, and reliable support systems that understand the non-linear nature of attachment healing.

CREATING LASTING TRANSFORMATION

Establishing lasting transformation in attachment patterns requires attention to internal and external maintenance strategies. This involves creating what attachment researchers call "islands of security"—reliable practices and relationships that support ongoing growth even during challenging periods.

The long-term success story of Mitchell and Susan, partners who identified with avoidant attachment, demonstrates the importance of creating sustainable change practices. After initial progress in therapy, they developed what they called their "secure connection protocol"—a set of daily and weekly practices designed to maintain their growth trajectory. This included daily check-ins about emotional states, weekly vulnerability practices, and monthly reviews of their attachment progress. Importantly, they built flexibility into their system, recognizing that different periods of life require different levels of active attention to attachment work.

Training the nervous system for lasting change requires what neuroscientists call "repetition in novelty," which means practicing new connection patterns in varying contexts and situations. Dr. Rachel Goldman's research on attachment transformation highlights the importance of gradually expanding the contexts in which we practice secure attachment behaviors. This might begin with practicing new patterns in therapy, then with close friends, and eventually in more challenging relationships or situations.

INTEGRATION AND ONGOING GROWTH

The final phase of attachment work involves integrating new patterns so profoundly that they become our default way of relating. This integration process requires an understanding that attachment security is not a destination but a dynamic state that requires ongoing attention and care.

Professor Dr. Elizabeth Chen's forty-year study of attachment transformation reveals that individuals who achieve lasting change share specific characteristics in their approach to integration. They maintain what she calls "conscious attachment practice"—regular reflection on their patterns, ongoing engagement with growth opportunities, and active cultivation of secure relationships. Rather than seeing their attachment work as complete, they view it as an ongoing process of refinement and deepening.

The creation of a personal attachment legacy represents a powerful aspect of integration. This involves transforming our patterns and becoming secure attachment sources for others. William, a teacher who documented his attachment journey over fifteen years, discovered that his healing process enabled him to create more secure classroom environments for his students. His story demonstrates how personal attachment work can ripple outward, contributing to broader social transformation.

The journey of attachment transformation ultimately leads us toward what attachment theorist John Bowlby called "felt security" —a deep, embodied sense of safety in connection that allows for intimacy and autonomy. This state is not characterized by the absence of attachment activation but by our increased capacity to maintain connection through various emotional states and challenges. It represents not the end of our attachment journey but the beginning of a new way of being in a relationship with ourselves and others. With that in mind, let us now explore how we can make those first steps of change from avoidant to secure attachment.

CHAPTER 5
TRANSFORMING AVOIDANT PATTERNS THROUGH TRUST AND EMOTIONAL INTIMACY

TRANSFORMING AVOIDANT PATTERNS IS KEY TO DEEPENING connections in relationships. This chapter focuses on building mutual trust through honest communication and accountability, allowing people in various relationships to engage fully. We also explore the role of emotional intimacy in sharing thoughts and feelings, which helps dismantle barriers to connection. By practicing intentional exercises and fostering open dialogue, we can begin to build a safe space for vulnerability in our relationships.

FOUNDATION OF TRUST AFTER AVOIDANCE

Mutual trust, the cornerstone of any healthy relationship, is not a one-way street but a bridge that spans a vast chasm, connecting two worlds. This trust bridge, built on shared experiences and mutual understanding, allows both parties to be vulnerable without fear of betrayal, fostering deeper connections and greater intimacy. When trust is broken, it can feel as if the bridge has collapsed, leaving both parties stranded on opposite sides, struggling to find a way back to each other. Picture a couple sitting at their kitchen table, casually discussing their weekend plans. The ease of their conversation reflects a foundation of trust built over time through consistent honesty and shared understanding. These simple interactions highlight how trust is not built solely during significant events but in daily exchanges where partners feel safe to express themselves without fear of judgment. Trust often reveals itself in the small, everyday moments.

To cultivate trust, begin with consistent honesty and transparency. This means aligning your words with your actions, creating a reliable pattern on which others can depend. Transparency involves openly sharing your thoughts and feelings, even when they are difficult to express. By doing so, you eliminate secrecy and foster an environment where trust can flourish. Gradually opening up can be especially effective for those recovering from avoidant patterns. Vulnerability does not have to happen all at once—it can start with sharing a meaningful experience or expressing a minor worry. These small moments of openness invite your partner to do the same, slowly deepening the emotional connection.

Building the trust back up after breaking it requires patience and conscious effort. You can begin with sincere apologies and accountability. Acknowledge the harm caused and take responsibility for your actions without making excuses. Let the person know you understand your behavior's impact and are committed to making amends. Being transparent about your intentions and motivations can also prevent misunderstandings from escalating. When you explain why you made a particular decision or how you feel about a situation, you offer clarity that strengthens trust. Open conversations about misunderstandings help both partners feel seen and understood, reinforcing the relationship's stability. Along the same lines, mutual understanding, the ability to comprehend and respect each other's perspectives, is vital in trust-building. It helps resolve conflicts and make decisions that benefit both parties.

Establishing and respecting personal boundaries is another crucial aspect of trust-building. Clearly communicating your limits—such as needing alone time or identifying sensitive topics—helps your partner understand and respect your needs. Likewise, honoring your partner's boundaries shows you value their autonomy. This mutual respect fosters a safe space where trust can naturally grow. Another vital step is following through on promises and commitments. When you say you will do something, ensure that you follow through. This consistency builds reliability, reinforcing the belief that you are dependable. As time passes, these small acts of honesty and reliability form the bedrock of trust, creating a strong and lasting foundation for your relationships.

Implementing trust-building rituals or activities can also help restore the connection. These might include regular check-ins, where you discuss your feelings and progress, or shared activities that strengthen your bond, like going for a walk or cooking a meal together. For instance, you could set aside a specific weekly time for a "trust-building talk" where you openly share your feelings and concerns. Or you could plan a "trust-building day" where you engage in activities that require teamwork and cooperation, such as a cooking challenge or a DIY project. These rituals provide a structured way to rebuild trust, offering tangible steps toward healing and reconciliation. Remember, rebuilding trust takes time, but restoring the bridge that once connected you is possible with effort and dedication.

Mutual trust is essential for the health and longevity of any relationship. Trust-building should never be a one-sided effort; it requires the active participation of both parties. Encourage open dialogue about trust issues, creating a space where both people feel safe to express their concerns and needs. This dialogue fosters mutual understanding and allows you to address the problems before they escalate. But how do you engage in these open discussions effectively? Start by setting aside a particular time to talk about trust, ensuring that both of you are in a calm and receptive state of mind. As we talked about in Chapter 2, use "I" statements like "I feel...," "I need...," or "I am concerned about..." to express your feelings and concerns, and actively listen to the other person's perspective without interrupting. Collaborating on trust-building exercises can further enhance this process. Consider engaging in activities requiring teamwork and cooperation, strengthening the relationship. These exercises can take many forms, from problem-solving tasks like planning a trip to shared hobbies like cooking a meal together, each offering an opportunity to work together toward a common goal. By nurturing mutual trust, you create a resilient bond capable of withstanding the challenges that inevitably arise in relationships.

Reflection Section: Trust-Building Checklist

This section provides questions to help you evaluate and enhance trust in your relationships. By reflecting on these questions often, you can ensure your trust-building efforts remain steady and effective.

- **Openness Audit**: Do you share your thoughts and feelings transparently?
- **Apology Acknowledgment**: Have you taken responsibility for past mistakes?
- **Consistency Check**: Are your actions aligned with your words?
- **Commitment Review**: Are you following through on promises?
- **Mutual Dialogue**: Are you engaging in open discussions about trust?

Use this checklist to evaluate and enhance trust in your relationships. Regular reflection can help you remain on track and ensure your trust-building efforts remain steady and effective. Please take a few moments to consider these questions and reflect on how you can apply the insights to your relationships.

INITIAL STEPS IN EMOTIONAL CONNECTION

Imagine sitting with someone you care about deeply, feeling the warmth that comes from their presence and the profound connection you share. This is emotional intimacy at its core—a closeness transcending physical presence and tapping into what it truly means to know and understand another person. Emotional intimacy—a deep bond beyond physical interactions—is essential for relationship satisfaction. It enables individuals to express their deepest thoughts, feelings, and dreams. It is the kind of bond where you feel seen and understood, creating a profound sense of safety and acceptance.

This level of intimacy plays a crucial role in relationship satisfaction, as it helps build trust and empathy, fostering more substantial, more resilient relationships. When emotional intimacy is present, it is a glue that holds relationships together, providing the emotional support needed to weather life's ups and downs. It allows people, especially partners, to navigate challenges with a united front, enhancing individual and collective well-being. The benefits of emotional intimacy are manifold, leading to deeper connections that enrich your relational experiences and contribute to a fulfilling life. Emotional intimacy is built through shared emotional experiences—laughter, tears, or even comfortable silence—that weave a fabric of trust and understanding. These shared moments create a safe space where both individuals feel valued, accepted, and deeply connected.

Enhancing emotional closeness can be achieved through intentional exercises encouraging openness and empathy. One simple yet powerful practice is sharing daily highs and lows with your partner, family member, or friend. Set aside time each day to discuss the moments that brought joy and those that were challenging. This exercise fosters communication and offers a window into each other's emotional worlds, deepening understanding and connection. Another effective exercise is practicing active empathy through shared experiences. This involves engaging in activities requiring collaboration and support, such as cooking a meal, taking a class, or volunteering together. These shared experiences create a bond because they require you to work together, understand each other's needs, and support each other, strengthening your emotional connection and fostering emotional intimacy. Another powerful method to deepen emotional intimacy is sharing personal narratives and life stories. Take turns recounting experiences that have shaped who you are, from childhood memories to significant life events. This practice allows partners, family members, or friends to explore more profound layers of each other's personalities, fostering empathy and a stronger emotional bond.

Despite its benefits, emotional intimacy often encounters barriers that can hinder its development. Fear of judgment or rejection is a common obstacle, preventing individuals from opening up fully. To overcome this, it is vital to create an environment where both people feel safe to express themselves without fear of criticism. Start by acknowledging these fears and discussing them openly with the other person. This dialogue can help dispel misconceptions and build a foundation of trust. It is also essential to actively listen and validate the other person's feelings without judgment. Affirming and validating the other person's emotions is equally important in creating emotional safety. Acknowledge their feelings as real and significant, even if they differ from your perspective. This validation nurtures a secure environment where both people feel comfortable expressing themselves openly, deepening the foundation of trust in the relationship.

To foster a safe space for emotional expression, you could establish "emotional safety rules" such as no interrupting, judgment, or dismissive responses. Gradually opening up emotionally can also be achieved through incremental sharing, where you begin with small disclosures and progressively increase the depth as comfort grows. This method lets you test the waters and build confidence in sharing and vulnerability. Over months, these steps can begin to help dismantle the barriers to emotional intimacy, paving the way for a richer, more connected relationship.

Maintaining emotional intimacy is not a one-time task. It is an ongoing effort. It requires a commitment to nurturing the connection. Regular check-ins with other people, especially partners, are essential to sustaining this intimacy. Schedule time to discuss your feelings, needs, and goals, ensuring you remain aligned and connected. These check-ins provide an opportunity to address any concerns and celebrate successes, reinforcing the bond between you and providing a sense of reassurance and connection. Taking part in activities that promote emotional bonding is another effective way to maintain intimacy. Consider embarking on new adventures together, whether exploring a hobby, traveling to a new destination, or volunteering for a cause you both care about. These shared experiences create lasting memories and deepen your connection, continually strengthening the emotional intimacy that forms the heart of your relationship.

DEVELOPING HEALTHY COMMUNICATION SKILLS

Imagine trying to tune a radio to a clear station amid static. This is what communication can feel like when avoidant patterns are at play. Effective communication is the tool that cuts through the noise, allowing clarity and understanding to emerge. It is pivotal in transforming these patterns into secure attachments where both people feel heard and valued. Through communication, conflicts can be resolved not by who speaks the loudest but by who listens the best. It enhances understanding by allowing you to see the world through the other person's eyes, fostering empathy and connection. When communication flows freely, it becomes the bridge between trust and intimacy travel.

Practical communication techniques can transform how you connect with others. As mentioned, one such method involves using "I" statements to express feelings without casting blame. Instead of saying, "You never listen to me," try, "I feel unheard when we don't discuss things." This shifts the focus from blame to personal experience, reducing defensiveness and opening the door to dialogue. Active listening is equally crucial. It means fully concentrating on what the other person is saying and reflecting their words back to them to confirm understanding. This might sound like, "So, you're saying you felt left out when I went out with friends?" Reflective responses demonstrate your engagement and empathy, building deeper connections through sincere exchanges.

Communication pitfalls often trip us up, leading to misunderstandings and conflicts. Avoiding assumptions and mind-reading is vital. It is easy to assume you know what the other person is thinking, but this often leads to miscommunication. Instead, ask clarifying questions to ensure you are on the same page. Managing defensiveness is another common hurdle. When criticized, the natural reaction is often to defend ourselves. However, by taking a moment to breathe and consider the feedback, you can respond thoughtfully rather than reactively. This approach fosters a more constructive and open dialogue, allowing for growth and understanding. Criticism can be hard to hear, but it often holds the key to unlocking deeper understanding when approached with an open mind.

Practice is key to building these communication skills. Role-playing difficult conversations can provide a safe space to explore and refine your communication techniques. Think of a challenging topic and take turns playing each other's roles. This exercise helps you understand The other person's perspective and offers insight into your communication style. Exercises in expressing needs and boundaries can further enhance your skills. Practice articulating what you need from the other person, whether it is more quality time or space to pursue personal interests. Clearly stating your boundaries and needs invites mutual understanding and respect, laying a foundation for a healthier relationship dynamic.

Interactive Element: Communication Role-Play Exercise

- **Scenario Setup**: Choose a familiar conflict, like differing plans for the weekend.
- **Role-Swap**: Partner A expresses their needs using "I" statements while Partner B actively listens and reflects.
- **Switch Roles**: Partner B shares their perspective, and Partner A practices active listening.
- **Debrief**: Discuss what felt challenging and what was learned.

Use this exercise to explore communication dynamics and discover new ways to connect. Practicing these techniques in a controlled setting helps build confidence, making applying them in real-life situations easier. Remember, effective communication is a skill. It grows with practice and patience, leading to more secure and satisfying relationships.

MANAGING EMOTIONAL DETACHMENT

Emotional detachment is often a protective shield, guarding against the discomfort of vulnerability. It is a defense mechanism to cope with past wounds or present uncertainties. For some, this detachment feels like a safe harbor where emotions cannot overwhelm or hurt. However, this can create an invisible barrier in relationships, leaving partners, family members, or friends feeling isolated and unsupported. The warmth of connection fades when one partner feels emotionally absent, and the relationship can suffer. Significant others may feel they are reaching out to someone who is no longer there, leading to feelings of neglect and loneliness. This emotional distance can chip away at the foundation of support and understanding vital for a thriving relationship.

Re-engaging emotionally requires a conscious effort to reconnect with your feelings. As mentioned, mindfulness practices can be particularly effective, helping you become more present in your emotional experiences. Mindfulness lets you observe your emotions without judgment by focusing on the here and now, encouraging you to feel rather than suppress. Consider putting aside a few minutes daily to engage in mindfulness meditation, focusing on your breathing and body sensations. This practice can help you connect better with your emotions, fostering a sense of presence that counteracts detachment. Journaling is another valuable tool in this process. By writing down your feelings and thoughts, you can explore and articulate emotions that might otherwise remain unexamined. Journaling provides a safe space to process experiences and reflect on how they affect your emotional landscape, offering insights into patterns and triggers.

Emotional regulation plays an essential role in managing detachment. It involves recognizing and naming emotions as they arise, a skill that can help prevent feelings from becoming overwhelming. Start by identifying what you are feeling in the moment and giving it a name—whether it is anger, sadness, or joy. This simple labeling can create distance between you and your emotions, allowing you to respond rather than react. Breathing exercises can also support emotional regulation. Breathe slow and deep to calm your nervous system when emotions intensify. This practice can help reduce the urge to detach, making staying engaged with your feelings and those around you easier.

Getting support from loved ones is another crucial step in re-engaging emotionally. Sharing your experiences with others you trust can provide validation and perspective, helping you feel less alone. Seek out a person you trust, whether a friend or family member. Talk to them about what you are going through and ask for their support as you work on reconnecting with your emotions. Their feedback can offer insights into how detachment affects relationships, clarifying what needs to change. Involving others in your process can create a sense of accountability, encouraging you to stay committed to your emotional growth. Trusted individuals can offer encouragement and celebrate your progress, reinforcing your efforts to re-engage emotionally.

Interactive Element: Emotional Awareness Exercise

- **Daily Emotion Check-In**: Spend five minutes each day identifying and naming your emotions.
- **Journaling Prompt**: Reflect on a recent experience that triggered emotional detachment. What emotions were present? How did you respond?
- **Mindfulness Practice**: Set a timer for three minutes and focus on your breath, noticing any emotions that arise without judgment.

These exercises can help you become more attuned to your emotional state, promoting engagement and connection in your relationships. Regular practice can transform emotional detachment from a protective mechanism into an opportunity for growth and deeper understanding. Embracing your emotions and seeking support opens the door to more prosperous, fulfilling relationships.

EMBRACING VULNERABILITY IN RELATIONSHIPS

Vulnerability in relationships often gets a bad rap, yet it is one of the most profound elements that lead to genuine connections. To be vulnerable means to open yourself up to reveal parts of yourself that are tender and true. It is not about exposing weaknesses but about sharing your authentic self, warts, and all. This openness creates a pathway to genuine connection, allowing you to experience deeper intimacy with the other person. When you allow someone to see you as you truly are, you invite them to do the same, fostering a mutual understanding that forms the bedrock of secure attachment. There is a paradox here. By embracing vulnerability, you actually become stronger. This strength comes not from putting up defenses but knowing that you can be open and still be okay. It is about resilience, about understanding that even if you stumble, you can get back up, and your relationship can weather the storm.

However, the notion of being vulnerable can evoke fear. The thought of laying bare your innermost thoughts and feelings can be daunting because the risk of judgment and rejection comes with it. Many fear that showing their vulnerabilities will be seen as weak or inadequate. This misconception often stems from societal norms that equate strength with stoicism and emotional self-reliance. Yet, true strength lies in the ability to stand firm in your truth and embrace and own your imperfections. It involves stepping into uncertainty with the courage to face whatever comes, knowing that vulnerability is not a liability but a powerful tool for connection.

To cultivate vulnerability, share personal stories and experiences with the other person. These narratives do not have to be epic tales; they can be simple anecdotes that reveal your desires, fears, or dreams. By sharing these pieces of yourself, you invite the other person into your world, allowing them to understand you on a deeper level. Practicing openness in everyday interactions can further encourage vulnerability. Instead of defaulting to surface-level conversations, challenge yourself to go deeper. When asked how your day was, instead of saying "fine," share the parts that mattered—the small victories, the frustrations, the moments that made you pause. By consistently practicing openness, you create a habit of vulnerability, making it a natural part of your interactions.

The rewards of embracing vulnerability are significant. For one, it deepens trust. When you show your true self, you tell the other person you fully trust them. This fosters a reciprocal trust, encouraging them to be open with you in return. As each layer of vulnerability is revealed, mutual understanding blossoms. You begin to see each other as allies on a shared path, navigating life's challenges together. Vulnerability also enhances emotional resilience. By facing your fears and opening up, you build a support network that bolsters you in times of need. This network provides a cushion, softening the blows of life's inevitable hardships. Knowing you have someone who sees and supports you in your most vulnerable moments gives you the strength to face whatever comes.

As this chapter closes, consider how vulnerability can transform your relationships. By embracing it, you pave the way for deeper connections built on a foundation of trust and mutual understanding. This sets the stage for creating secure attachments where love and resilience flourish together. Looking ahead, we will explore how these principles can apply broadly, fostering growth and fulfillment in all areas of life.

CHAPTER 6
BUILDING SECURE ATTACHMENTS

IMAGINE YOURSELF IN A BUSTLING AIRPORT, WITNESSING THE heartwarming reunions of travelers with their loved ones. The sheer joy and relief in their eyes tell a story of trust and connection that transcends words. This scene beautifully captures the essence of secure attachment—a bond characterized by trust, empathy, and effective communication. Secure attachment is the foundation of healthy relationships, offering safety and support for individuals to thrive. It fosters an environment where people feel appreciated and heard, promoting open and sincere communication. In contrast, insecure attachment styles, such as anxious or avoidant, can lead to miscommunication and emotional distance, often resulting in relationships fraught with tension and misunderstanding. You can build resilient, fulfilling, and enduring relationships by understanding and nurturing secure attachments.

FOUNDATIONS OF SECURE ATTACHMENT

As we discussed at the beginning of the book, secure attachment is rooted in psychological and emotional well-being. It begins with positive self-esteem and self-worth, enabling you to engage authentically and confidently with others. When you believe in your value, you approach relationships with openness and trust rather than fear and defensiveness. This self-assurance is the cornerstone of secure attachment, allowing you to express your needs without hesitation. Emotional regulation, a vital skill, plays a significant role in managing your emotions effectively. By recognizing and responding to your feelings in a balanced way, you can navigate conflicts and challenges with composure and empathy, feeling empowered and in control. This ability to regulate emotions is a hallmark of secure attachment, fostering stability and understanding in relationships. It is not just about managing conflicts but about feeling empowered to navigate them in a way that strengthens the relationship. These psychological and emotional elements create a framework for secure attachment, empowering you to connect with others in meaningful and lasting ways.

The development of secure attachment often begins in childhood and is influenced by early experiences with caregivers. Consistent and reliable caregiving provides security as children learn to trust their needs will be fulfilled. This trust forms the basis of secure attachment, allowing children to explore the world confidently. Positive reinforcement and emotional support from caregivers strengthen this bond, as children feel valued and loved. These nurturing experiences lay the groundwork for secure attachment, shaping how individuals perceive and engage in relationships. When caregivers respond sensitively and consistently, they instill a sense of safety and predictability, which fosters secure attachment. This early foundation helps individuals develop healthy relational patterns characterized by trust, empathy, and effective communication. Understanding the role of these early experiences can help us gain insight into our current attachment patterns and how we can work toward secure attachments, enlightening us and fostering self-awareness.

In adult relationships, secure attachment offers numerous benefits that enhance emotional resilience and satisfaction. Those with secure attachments are better equipped to handle stress and adversity, as they possess a stable foundation of self-worth and emotional regulation. This resilience allows them to navigate challenges gracefully and have a positive outlook even in difficult times. Secure attachment also contributes to greater satisfaction and longevity in relationships, as it fosters open communication and mutual support. People feel safe expressing their needs and emotions, knowing they will receive understanding and compassion. This creates a cycle of trust and intimacy, where both people feel valued and respected. The emotional resilience and satisfaction accompanying secure attachment lay the foundation for enduring relationships characterized by love, trust, and shared growth. These benefits are not out of reach but a potential that can be realized through understanding and nurturing secure attachments.

Reflection Section: Building Secure Attachments

- **Self-Assessment**: If you have not done so already, reflect on your current attachment style. Do you feel secure in your relationships, or do you often experience anxiety or avoidance? Consider how your early experiences may have influenced your attachment patterns.
- **Caregiver Influence**: Consider your caregivers and how their behavior shaped your understanding of relationships. How have these early experiences influenced your approach to attachment as an adult?
- **Emotional Regulation**: Practice mindful breathing or journaling techniques to enhance emotional regulation. How do these practices help you manage emotions in your relationships?
- **Building Trust**: Identify ways to build trust and empathy in your relationships. What steps can you take to foster open communication and mutual support?

Engaging with these reflections can help you understand your attachment style and work toward building secure attachments. As discussed in previous chapters, cultivating trust, empathy, and effective communication can create resilient and fulfilling relationships. We will continue to build on these principles by exploring these ideas more fully.

CULTIVATING A SECURE ATTACHMENT MINDSET

Imagine looking at relationships as a refuge, a place where support and security intertwine seamlessly. This perspective forms the core of a secure attachment mindset. Here, relationships are not burdens or obligations but sources of mutual strength and reassurance. Embracing this mindset means understanding that interdependence is not a sign of weakness but a healthy balance between autonomy and connection. It is about recognizing that you do not have to face life's challenges alone. You can rely on others while still standing firm in your identity. This balance fosters a sense of belonging, where both people contribute to each other's well-being. Seeing relationships in this light transforms them into partnerships where support flows both ways, creating a nurturing environment that encourages personal growth and shared happiness.

Cultivating this secure mindset begins with challenging negative beliefs about relationships. Many of us carry assumptions shaped by past experiences or societal pressures, such as the notion that needing help is a sign of dependency. Start by identifying these beliefs and questioning their validity. Are they based on reality, or are they remnants of past wounds? Replace these limiting notions with positive affirmations that reflect a healthier perspective. Tell yourself that seeking support is a strength, not a flaw. Practicing positive self-talk can reinforce these new beliefs. When doubt creeps in, remind yourself of your worth and the value you bring to your relationships. These affirmations can serve as anchors, keeping you grounded in a mindset that embraces interdependence and mutual support.

Self-awareness is vital in developing a secure attachment mindset. It involves reflecting on your relationship patterns and understanding how they were formed. Take time to identify insecurities that may hinder your ability to connect with others.

These insecurities might stem from past relationships or childhood experiences. By acknowledging them, you can begin the process of healing. Self-awareness allows you to see how these patterns influence your interactions, empowering you to make conscious choices that align with your desire for secure attachment. It provides clarity and insight, helping you navigate relationships with intention and authenticity. As you become more attuned to your internal landscape, you can address insecurities compassionately, paving the way for healthier connections.

A growth-oriented perspective encourages you to view relationships as dynamic entities that can evolve and adapt as years pass. Embrace change as a natural part of any partnership. Relationships are not static; they require flexibility and openness to thrive. Instead of fearing change, see it as an opportunity for growth and enrichment. Celebrate progress and small victories along the way. Acknowledge the milestones you reach together, whether they are emotional breakthroughs or shared achievements. These celebrations reinforce the bond between you and others, highlighting your journey together. This perspective fosters resilience, enabling you to navigate life's ups and downs with grace and unity. By cultivating a mindset that values growth, you create a solid base for lasting and fulfilling relationships.

As you work toward a secure attachment mindset, remember it is a continuous process. It is about embracing the complexities of relationships with an open heart and a willingness to learn. Each step forward, no matter how small, contributes to a deeper understanding of yourself and your connections with others.

ADVANCING TRUST IN SECURE RELATIONSHIPS

Imagine a couple sitting at their kitchen table, discussing their weekend plans effortlessly. Their conversation reflects a deep trust that has been nurtured over time. Advancing trust in a secure relationship involves more than just establishing it; it requires continual growth through consistent, honest communication and intentional actions.

Consistent and transparent communication remains the backbone of trust. Sharing significant thoughts and feelings openly while respecting personal boundaries reinforces the bond between partners. This does not require disclosing every minute detail of daily life but involves being forthcoming about meaningful matters. This level of openness signals that transparency is valued, creating an environment where trust deepens over time.

Reliability is equally essential in advancing trust. Continuously following through on promises—whether handling everyday tasks like picking up groceries or offering unwavering support during difficult times—strengthens the belief that one partner can depend on the other. This steady dependability reassures both partners, fostering a secure and trustworthy relationship foundation.

Deepening trust also involves a growing willingness to share personal thoughts and emotions. Gradual vulnerability invites deeper connection. Sharing experiences that evoke emotion or discussing personal challenges allows both partners to feel seen and understood. Couples cultivate a deeper emotional bond by encouraging this mutual vulnerability, solidifying their trust.

Transparency is not only about sharing thoughts but also about clarifying intentions and motivations. Explaining the reasons behind decisions or actions reduces misunderstandings and strengthens trust. Addressing any confusion or misinterpretation promptly shows a proactive commitment to the relationship. Open dialogue about misunderstandings reflects a dedication to maintaining clarity and mutual respect.

Respecting and adapting to each other's evolving boundaries further advances trust. As relationships grow, personal needs and comfort zones may shift. Regular discussions about individual boundaries—such as the need for personal space or sensitive topics—demonstrate care and respect for each other's autonomy. Honoring these boundaries reassures both partners that their emotional safety is a shared priority.

Advancing trust in secure relationships is a continuous process of intentional communication, reliability, vulnerability, transparency, and boundary respect. By nurturing these elements, couples can deepen their connection, reinforcing a resilient and lasting trust that evolves with the relationship.

MASTERING DEEP EMOTIONAL CONNECTION

Imagine sitting with someone you care about deeply, feeling the warmth that comes from their presence and the profound connection you share. This is emotional intimacy at its most transformative level—a closeness transcending physical presence and tapping into what it means to know and be known by another person. Deep emotional intimacy forms the bedrock of profound connection, creating a sacred space where both individuals can reveal their innermost thoughts, fears, and aspirations without judgment. It is cultivated through shared emotional experiences, those precious moments where shared laughter, witnessed tears, or comfortable silence weaves an unbreakable bond. These experiences create a tapestry of trust and understanding, fostering a deep sense of safety and validation.

When emotional intimacy reaches this master level, it becomes more than just the heartbeat of a relationship—it transforms into its very soul, nurturing a profound sense of belonging and mutual growth. This depth of connection requires dedicated practice and intention. Consider implementing advanced emotional connection exercises into your daily life. One powerful approach is establishing sacred emotional check-in rituals with significant others. These are not merely casual conversations but intentional spaces for deep exploration of feelings, dreams, and vulnerabilities. They might take the form of weekly reflection walks or dedicated evening connection sessions where phones are turned off and presence is prioritized.

The art of sharing personal narratives evolves at this level into what we might call "sacred storytelling"—taking turns not just recounting life experiences but exploring their more profound meaning and impact on your current patterns and beliefs. This practice reveals the multilayered nature of your personality and invites others into the complex tapestry of your inner world, fostering profound emotional bonds. These advanced exercises cultivate what psychologists call "radical vulnerability"—a state where both individuals feel safe enough to share surface-level emotions and their deepest fears, hopes, and authentic selves.

Creating an environment for this depth of emotional intimacy requires mastering several key elements. Active listening transforms into what we might call "soul listening"—where you're not just hearing words but sensing the underlying emotions, unspoken needs, and subtle nuances in communication. This deep, empathetic presence lets you connect with others almost intuitively, creating a space where they feel heard and truly understood.

The practice of validation evolves beyond simple acknowledgment into what we might call "emotional resonance," where one can recognize and deeply attune to another's emotional experience. This creates a profound sense of being emotionally held and understood, fostering the deepest levels of intimacy possible in human connection.

Managing barriers at this level involves recognizing that fear of vulnerability is not just about potential rejection but often connects to our deepest existential concerns about being indeed known. Working through these fears requires courage and a fundamental shift in how we view vulnerability—seeing it not as a risk to be managed but as the gateway to the most meaningful connections possible in our lives.

Mastering these elements makes emotional intimacy not just a component of our relationships but their very essence, creating profoundly healing and transforming growth-promoting connections. This mastery allows us to develop relationships characterized by extraordinary depth, authenticity, and mutual understanding.

LONG-TERM STRATEGIES FOR SECURE RELATIONSHIPS

Imagine watching a movie where two characters evolve over a period of time, their relationship deepening through countless shared experiences and challenges. This evolution mirrors the principles necessary for maintaining secure relationships. At its core lies a commitment to ongoing communication and connection. This does not mean endless conversations but regular, meaningful exchanges that keep both people in tune. It is about creating a rhythm of interaction where checking in becomes second nature. Whether it is a quick chat over breakfast or a more profound discussion at the end of the day, these interactions build a tapestry of understanding that strengthens the relationship. Prioritizing mutual respect and understanding is equally vital. It involves recognizing each other's perspectives and valuing them, even when they differ from yours. This respect fosters a climate of cooperation, where both people feel valued and heard, ensuring the relationship remains harmonious and resilient.

Securing relationship longevity requires practical strategies that adapt to the ebb and flow of life. Regularly revisiting and renegotiating relationship goals and boundaries is one such strategy. Life changes, and so do people. What worked in the past may no longer serve in the present. By periodically assessing your goals and boundaries, you ensure they remain relevant and supportive. This process involves open discussions where both people express their needs and aspirations, adjusting the relationship's trajectory as necessary. Engaging in shared activities that promote bonding is another way to sustain the relationship.

These activities might include hobbies, travel, or exploring new interests together. These shared experiences create memories and connections that enrich the relationship, reinforcing your bond.

Flexibility is the thread that weaves through these strategies, allowing relationships to adapt and flourish. Being open to change and new experiences together keeps the relationship dynamic and alive. It means embracing opportunities that arise, whether they are planned or spontaneous. This openness to change fosters a sense of adventure and growth, inviting both parties to explore and learn together. Adjusting to life transitions as a team further reinforces this flexibility. Life is full of unexpected turns, from career shifts to family changes. You strengthen the relationship's resilience by approaching these transitions as a united front. Supporting each other through these changes ensures that both people feel secure and valued, reinforcing the relationship's foundation of trust and cooperation.

Fostering a supportive partnership involves encouraging individual growth within the relationship. Each partner should feel free to pursue their interests and goals, knowing they have the support of their partner. This encouragement strengthens the individual's sense of self and enriches the relationship, as both bring new experiences and perspectives. Providing emotional and practical support during challenges is another key aspect of a supportive partnership. Whether offering a listening ear during a tough day or helping with practical tasks, this support reinforces the bond between partners. It shows a commitment to each other's well-being, creating a partnership where both individuals feel nurtured and secure.

As we close this chapter, remember that secure relationships require consistent effort and adaptability. Committing to ongoing communication, embracing flexibility, and fostering a supportive partnership lays the groundwork for a resilient and deeply fulfilling relationship. Building and maintaining secure attachments is a continuing process with opportunities for growth and connection. The following chapter will explore how these principles can create even deeper emotional bonds and a more profound sense of intimacy in our many different relationships.

CHAPTER 7
NAVIGATING DIFFERENT RELATIONSHIP CONTEXTS

NAVIGATING RELATIONSHIPS CAN BE PARTICULARLY CHALLENGING FOR individuals with avoidant attachment styles. This chapter explores the complex dynamics at play, beginning with the unique hurdles faced during the dating process. We delve into the intricacies of developing romantic intimacy, highlighting the gradual approach necessary for those who fear vulnerability while also craving connection. Furthermore, we examine the profound impact of rejection sensitivity, illustrating how past experiences can shape present interactions and relationships. Family systems often mirror these attachment patterns, presenting both the origins of avoidant behavior and opportunities for healing. Finally, we discuss creating new family dynamics that foster emotional availability and connection. Each section offers examples, insights, and strategies for understanding and overcoming the challenges of avoidant attachment, ultimately paving the way for healthier relationships.

DATING WITH AVOIDANT ATTACHMENT

The dating landscape can be particularly daunting for individuals with avoidant attachment patterns. The early stages of a romantic connection often trigger intense attachment system activation, leading to a push-pull dynamic that can perplex both parties.

"Attachment system activation" refers to the psychological process by which individuals seek comfort and connection from significant others, particularly during stress or distress. This concept is rooted in the attachment theory we discussed in Chapter 1. When individuals experience feelings of threat or insecurity, their attachment system is activated, prompting them to reach out for support from those they feel bonded with, such as partners, family members, or close friends. The activation of this system can influence behavior, emotions, and decisions, driving individuals to seek proximity and comfort from loved ones to cope with anxiety or uncertainty. It plays a vital role in relationships and overall emotional well-being.

We can look at one woman's dating journey, which illustrates some common patterns. After several promising relationships ended due to Lisa's unconscious withdrawal at signs of deepening intimacy, she began working with an attachment-informed dating coach. Together, they developed strategies for maintaining connection during activation, including transparent communication about her need for space and structured check-ins with potential partners.

Establishing dating boundaries is a delicate art that requires a balance between protection and connection. This might involve setting clear expectations about communication frequency, planning dates with built-in alone time, and developing scripts for discussing attachment needs early in relationships. The aim is not to eliminate attachment activation but to make it manageable and conducive to personal growth.

MANAGING REJECTION SENSITIVITY

The fear of rejection often lies at the heart of avoidant attachment patterns, creating a complex web of protective behaviors that paradoxically increase the likelihood of experiencing rejection. Understanding rejection sensitivity requires examining how early experiences of emotional unavailability or inconsistent caregiving create heightened vigilance to potential abandonment.

The transformation of Karen, a marketing executive, illustrates how rejection sensitivity can be effectively managed. Early in her career, Karen interpreted any constructive feedback as a personal rejection, leading her to maintain an emotional distance from colleagues and miss mentorship opportunities. Through dedicated work with her therapist, she developed what she called her "rejection resilience toolkit." This included techniques for distinguishing between genuine rejection and perceived threats and strategies for maintaining connection during periods of heightened sensitivity.

Building rejection resilience involves a crucial understanding that not all disconnections signify rejection. When Thomas, a graduate student, began examining his rejection sensitivity, he discovered that his automatic interpretation of unanswered text messages as rejection stemmed from childhood experiences of emotional neglect. Through mindful awareness practice, he learned to pause before acting on these interpretations, creating space for alternative explanations and more measured responses.

BUILDING ROMANTIC INTIMACY

Developing romantic intimacy with an avoidant attachment style requires a gradual, intentional approach that honors the need for connection and the fear of vulnerability. This process involves creating what attachment theorist John Bowlby called a "secure base" to explore deeper intimacy levels.

The successful journey of partners David and Jason demonstrates this approach. Both identifying with avoidant attachment patterns, they initially struggled with emotional intimacy. Through couples therapy, they developed a practice they called "scheduled vulnerability"—setting aside specific times for deeper emotional sharing while maintaining clear boundaries around alone time. This structure provided the safety needed to increase their capacity for intimacy gradually.

Physical intimacy and attachment intertwine in complex ways for individuals with avoidant patterns. The body's response to physical closeness can trigger attachment activation, leading to withdrawal after intimate encounters. Understanding this connection allows for developing strategies to maintain an emotional presence during physical intimacy.

FAMILY RELATIONSHIPS AND ATTACHMENT HEALING

The family system often serves as both the source of avoidant attachment patterns and a crucial arena for healing. Working with family relationships requires understanding that current tensions usually reflect multi-generational patterns of emotional distance and unmet attachment needs.

Maria's work with her family demonstrates the complexity of this healing process. Growing up in a family that prided itself on emotional stoicism, Maria struggled to connect with her teenage daughter, who openly expressed emotional needs. Through family therapy, Maria discovered that her avoidant patterns reflected her grandmother's survival strategy during times of war—emotional distance had once served as protection but now hindered family connection. This understanding allowed Maria to begin bridging the generational gap, creating new patterns of emotional availability for her daughter.

Setting boundaries within family systems requires particular finesse when working with avoidant attachment. These boundaries must serve dual purposes: protecting against overwhelming emotional demands while remaining permeable enough for genuine connection. The process involves communicating needs while remaining open to family members' emotional responses.

CREATING NEW FAMILY DYNAMICS

Transforming family patterns requires sustained effort and patience from all involved members. Each small change in communication or behavior can create ripple effects throughout the family system, sometimes meeting resistance before leading to positive change.

The Johnson family's experience exemplifies this transformative process. When the eldest son, Robert, began addressing his avoidant attachment patterns in therapy, he initially faced resistance from family members accustomed to their emotionally distant dynamic. The family's breakthrough came during a holiday gathering when Robert shared his journey using the metaphor of a bridge built slowly over troubled waters. This image helped his family understand the challenge and the possibility of creating new connection patterns.

Fostering healthy connections within the family system involves creating what attachment theorists call "earned secure attachment." This process requires consistent, small steps toward greater emotional availability, with each family member moving at their own pace while remaining committed to a deeper connection.

PROFESSIONAL RELATIONSHIPS AND ATTACHMENT

The workplace often uniquely triggers attachment patterns, particularly for individuals with avoidant attachment styles who may have developed high achievement as a compensation strategy. Understanding how attachment manifests in professional settings allows for more effective navigation of workplace relationships while maintaining appropriate boundaries.

Dr. Sarah Martinez's research with corporate leaders revealed how avoidant attachment patterns often manifest as workaholism or difficulty delegating tasks. By studying successful executives who had addressed their attachment patterns, she identified key strategies for maintaining professional effectiveness while developing more secure relationship patterns. These strategies emphasized the importance of mentorship, clear communication about work boundaries, and regular check-ins with team members.

Leadership roles present particular challenges for individuals with avoidant attachment, as they require maintaining professional authority and fostering secure connections within teams. The experience of James, a tech startup founder, demonstrates how awareness of attachment patterns can enhance leadership effectiveness. James developed protocols for staying engaged during challenging conversations by understanding his tendency to withdraw during team conflicts, ultimately creating a more psychologically safe environment for his entire organization.

CHAPTER 8
CONFLICT RESOLUTION AND RELATIONSHIP GROWTH

REMEMBER WHEN A DISAGREEMENT WITH A PARTNER, FAMILY MEMBER, or friend seemed impossible to overcome? The tension, frustration, and the feeling of being misunderstood may still be vivid. But what if I told you that these conflicts are not just hurdles but potential stepping stones to deeper connections and personal growth? This chapter presents a structured approach to conflict resolution that respects both parties' needs and fosters mutual understanding. By approaching conflicts with intention, you can turn them into opportunities for building stronger, healthier relationships.

UNDERSTANDING THE ROOT CAUSES OF CONFLICT

Resolving conflicts effectively begins with identifying the root cause. Often, disagreements on the surface mask deeper issues related to unmet needs or unexpressed emotions. For example, an argument about household chores might stem from feelings of imbalance or underappreciation. The sense of relief and empowerment gained through understanding these underlying issues can be enlightening. To pinpoint the root cause, open a dialogue with the other person where you both express underlying concerns. Ask questions beyond the immediate conflict, such as, "What do you need from me in this situation?" or "How does this make you feel?" By exploring these deeper issues, you can address the real problem rather than just the symptoms.

Once you understand the underlying issues, it is crucial to establish common goals for resolution. A shared objective might be to ensure that both people feel heard and respected or to find a compromise that meets everyone's needs. For instance, in a disagreement about household chores, a common goal could be establishing a fair division of labor that both parties agree on. Framing the conflict resolution process as a collaborative effort encourages cooperation and reduces defensiveness. When both parties work toward a common goal, the focus shifts from winning the argument to finding a solution that benefits the relationship. This mindset fosters a sense of partnership and shared responsibility, paving the way for more constructive discussions and a more profound understanding of connection.

Maintaining a calm and open mindset is essential when navigating conflicts. Emotional reactions often escalate tensions, making it challenging to communicate effectively. Instead, practice techniques that manage these reactions, such as taking deep breaths or pausing to collect your thoughts before responding. This reassures you that you are in control of the situation. Creating a safe space for open discussion also helps. Choose a time and place where both parties can talk without distractions or interruptions. Set ground rules that encourage respectful dialogue, such as allowing each person to speak without interruption and agreeing to listen with an open mind. These practices create an environment where both people feel safe to express themselves honestly.

Compromise and collaboration are essential to resolving conflicts in a way that strengthens relationships. Rather than adopting a win-lose mentality, strive for mutually beneficial solutions. This might involve finding middle ground or creating new options that neither party initially considered. Encourage collaborative problem-solving by brainstorming solutions together. Ask questions like, "How can we address both of our needs?" or "What are some alternatives we haven't explored?" This approach resolves the immediate conflict and builds trust and cooperation.

Conflict Resolution Checklist

- **Preparation**: Reflect on your feelings and identify the root cause of the conflict.
- **Setting**: Select a peaceful and private environment for the discussion.
- **Mindset**: Approach the conversation with an open mind and a willingness to listen.
- **Dialogue**: Express your needs using "I" statements and listen to the other person's perspective without interrupting.
- **Common Goals**: Identify shared objectives for resolution.

- **Compromise**: Brainstorm solutions that address both parties' needs.
- **Agreement**: Agree on actionable steps to move forward.

This checklist is a practical guide to navigating conflicts with intention and care. Following these steps, you can transform disagreements into opportunities for growth and deeper connection. With practice, this process becomes second nature, enhancing the health and longevity of your relationships.

THE CRUCIAL ROLE OF ACTIVE LISTENING AND EMPATHY EXERCISES IN CONFLICT RESOLUTION

Imagine a conversation where you feel truly heard. Your words are acknowledged and understood as if the other person has stepped into your shoes. This is the power of active listening—a crucial skill in resolving conflicts and fostering more profound connections. Active listening reduces misunderstandings and miscommunications, which often arise when we listen to respond rather than to understand. When you practice active listening, you validate the other person's perspective, showing them that their thoughts and feelings matter. This validation can dissolve tension, opening the door to meaningful dialogue and resolution.

To enhance your active listening skills, consider engaging in exercises that focus on reflective listening. This technique involves paraphrasing what the other person says and confirming your understanding before responding. For instance, if the other person shares a frustration, you might say, "So, you're feeling overwhelmed because of the work deadlines." This reflection shows that you are paying attention and allows you to correct any misinterpretations. Another effective practice is honing your nonverbal communication cues. Nonverbal signals like maintaining eye contact, nodding, or leaning slightly forward indicate engagement and interest. These cues reassure the other person that you are present and attentive, reinforcing your connection.

Empathy has a crucial role in building and maintaining connections. It involves putting yourself in another's shoes and seeing the world through their eyes. This perspective shift fosters understanding, allowing you to connect with their emotions and experiences deeply. Empathy bridges gaps that words cannot, creating a shared emotional experience that strengthens bonds. Techniques for cultivating empathy include empathy mapping exercises, where you explore another person's feelings, thoughts, and motivations. In an empathy mapping exercise, you consider what the other person might feel, think, and want. Consider writing down what you believe the other person is experiencing, then discuss it with them to gain a clearer understanding. This exercise encourages open communication and mutual understanding, laying the groundwork for a more empathetic relationship.

To keep empathy alive in your relationships, it is crucial to practice it regularly. Daily empathy reflections can be a simple yet powerful tool. Spend a few minutes each day reflecting on your interactions. Ask yourself how you demonstrated empathy and where you might improve. This reflection helps internalize empathetic behaviors, making them a natural part of your interactions. Partner empathy challenges can also strengthen these skills. Set aside time with your partner to discuss each other's perspectives on various topics, challenging yourselves to see through each other's eyes. This practice enhances empathy and deepens your connection. It helps cultivate a relationship built on mutual understanding and respect. You can also practice this with other significant relationships you may have.

THE IMPORTANCE OF SETTING REALISTIC RELATIONSHIP EXPECTATIONS

In relationships, expectations guide how we interact and what we anticipate from others. They shape our perceptions and influence our satisfaction. Realistic expectations are vital because they help us navigate relationships without unnecessary disappointment or frustration. When expectations align with reality, they foster a sense of balance and understanding. On the other hand, unrealistic expectations can lead to repeated feelings of letdown. For instance, expecting the other person always to know precisely what you need without expressing it sets both of you up for failure. This expectation ignores that everyone has different perspectives and that open communication is necessary. Setting realistic expectations creates a foundation for a healthy relationship where both people feel valued and understood.

Understanding what you expect from a relationship starts with self-reflection. Take time to think about what you truly need and want from the other person. Reflective journaling can be a helpful tool in this process. Write down your thoughts on a fulfilling relationship, considering communication, support, and shared activities. Once you have a clearer picture, discuss these expectations with the other person. This dialogue is crucial because it reveals whether your visions align and where adjustments may be needed. By articulating your needs and listening to and acknowledging the other person's needs, you can work together to create a relationship that meets both of your expectations.

Unrealistic expectations can strain a relationship. They often stem from idealized notions of how a relationship should be, influenced by media, past experiences, or societal pressures. Common unrealistic expectations include believing that conflicts should never occur, that people should always agree, or that love alone can solve all problems. These expectations overlook the complexity and effort required to maintain a healthy relationship. When expectations go unmet, disappointment and resentment can grow. You might start to see the other person as inadequate or feel unfulfilled, which can lead to conflict or even the dissolution of the relationship. Recognizing and addressing these unrealistic expectations is crucial for maintaining harmony and satisfaction.

Modifying your expectations can lead to a more satisfying relationship. Start by setting achievable relationship goals that consider both peoples' needs and limitations. These goals may include spending quality time together weekly or improving communication by having regular check-ins. Practicing acceptance and flexibility is also key. Understand that no relationship is perfect, and both people will have strengths and weaknesses. Accepting this reality allows you to appreciate the other person for who they are rather than who you want them to be. Flexibility in your expectations means being open to change and adapting as the relationship evolves. This adaptability can strengthen your bond and create a more resilient relationship.

OVERCOMING PERFECTIONISM IN RELATIONSHIPS

Perfectionism in relationships often manifests as the pressure to meet unattainable standards for yourself and the other person. This drive for flawlessness can lead to constant dissatisfaction, as pursuing perfection leaves little room for the natural imperfections that characterize human interactions. Minor issues can become magnified—for example, a partner might criticize an unwashed dish or an unsaid compliment, not because these things matter in themselves but because they symbolize a broader failure to meet an unattainable ideal. Over time, this relentless pursuit of perfection can trigger conflicts, erode intimacy, and create a disconnect as the focus shifts from appreciating each other's unique qualities to critiquing perceived flaws.

Examining the root causes of perfectionism can provide insight into its impact on relationships. Fear of rejection or failure often underlies perfectionist tendencies, driven by a deep-seated belief that being imperfect equates to being unworthy. These internalized beliefs about worthiness and success may come from past experiences—such as childhood environments where love or approval seemed conditional on achievement—or societal pressures that idolize flawlessness. Recognizing these sources is the first step in addressing perfectionism. By understanding where these beliefs originated, individuals can begin to challenge their validity and reframe their perspective on what it means to be in a healthy, fulfilling relationship.

Challenging perfectionist thoughts requires intentional effort, reflection, and self-compassion. Cognitive restructuring techniques can help reframe negative thoughts about imperfection. When perfectionist thoughts arise, such as *I must do this perfectly*, or *I've failed*, pause and ask whether this belief is realistic or helpful. Consider alternative perspectives, like *doing my best is enough* or *imperfections are part of being human*. Similarly, when dwelling on a perceived flaw in your partner or loved one, pause and ask whether this thought is based on reality or an unrealistic standard. Practicing self-compassion is also essential— treat yourself with the understanding and kindness you would give a friend. Celebrate small successes and progress, focusing on effort rather than outcome. This shift in thinking can create a more positive and supportive environment where people feel accepted and valued for who they are rather than what they think they should be.

Embracing imperfection as a growth opportunity can transform the dynamics of a relationship. Instead of viewing mistakes as failures, see them as chances to learn and connect on a deeper level. When a misstep occurs, approach it with curiosity rather than criticism. Ask the other person how they perceived the situation and share your perspective. This open dialogue fosters empathy and understanding, strengthening your bond. Celebrate the progress you and your partner, family member, or friend make together, acknowledging the growth from facing challenges as a team. Focus on the journey of development rather than the destination of perfection, appreciating the unique qualities and strengths each of you brings to the relationship. By shifting focus from striving for perfection to valuing authenticity and effort, you create a space where love can flourish, unencumbered by unrealistic expectations.

CREATING A GROWTH-ORIENTED RELATIONSHIP PLAN

When you focus on growth within your relationships, you create dynamic ones that can evolve over the years. This approach not only enhances satisfaction but also increases longevity. You build resilience and adaptability by emphasizing growth, equipping both people to handle life's inevitable changes. A growth-oriented mindset encourages mutual support, allowing each person to develop individually while strengthening the relationship as a whole. You become allies in each other's journeys, fostering an environment where both can thrive. This mutual development creates a robust foundation to weather challenges and celebrate successes together.

To develop a personalized growth plan, set specific, measurable relationship goals. These might include improving communication, spending more quality time together, or supporting each other's aspirations. Determine what success is for each goal. Then, realistic timelines can be set to achieve them. When goals are clear and measurable, they become more attainable, providing motivation and direction. Next, identify areas for improvement and collaboration. Discuss openly where the relationship thrives and where it might need more attention. Perhaps you both agree that you want to enhance your emotional intimacy or work on better conflict resolution. Make these areas a focus in your growth plan, outlining actionable steps you can take together to address them.

Monitoring progress is crucial to any growth plan. Regular relationship check-ins allow you to reflect on your journey and adjust your goals as needed. Schedule time for these discussions, ensuring they are safe for honest communication. During these check-ins, celebrate milestones and progress. Recognizing successes, no matter how small, reinforces positive behavior and keeps momentum. Consider keeping a progress journal where you document these reflections and celebrations. This journal is a tangible reminder of your commitment to growth and can encourage you during challenging times. By tracking your progress, you gain insight into what works and needs adjustment, ensuring your growth plan remains relevant and practical.

Fostering a mindset of continuous improvement is vital to maintaining growth. Embrace change and view it as an opportunity for learning. Life has many unexpected events, and a growth-oriented approach prepares you to adapt gracefully. Encourage each other to seek new experiences and challenges individually and together. This shared pursuit of growth keeps the relationship fresh and exciting, especially for couples. Cultivating a supportive and encouraging environment is equally important. Celebrate each other's successes and offer support during setbacks. Create a relationship culture where growth is not only expected but eagerly anticipated. This positive atmosphere inspires both people to strive for their best selves, individually and together.

Integrating these strategies into your relationship lays the groundwork for a thriving relationship built on mutual growth and development. This approach enhances your connection and sets the stage for a more fulfilling future. By focusing on growth, you ensure that your relationship remains vibrant and resilient, equipped to handle whatever comes your way. In the next chapter, we will explore how building secure attachments is the natural progression from this growth-focused mindset, leading to deeper connections and lasting happiness.

CHAPTER 9
INTEGRATING SELF-DISCOVERY WITH THERAPEUTIC SUPPORT

PICTURE YOURSELF STANDING AT THE EDGE OF A VAST FOREST. EACH tree represents a different aspect of your emotional landscape; some are familiar, and others are mysterious. Venturing into this forest alone can be daunting and overwhelming. This is where therapy comes into play, offering a guiding hand and a reliable map to navigate the complexities of your emotional world. Therapy provides a supportive and structured space where you can safely explore and transform your attachment styles, helping you understand how early experiences shape your present interactions. It is a process that invites you to delve into your emotions and empowers you, uncovering patterns that may have gone unnoticed and discovering pathways to more secure connections.

WHEN AND WHY TO SEEK SUPPORT

Therapy is a platform for building trust, not only with the therapist but also with yourself. The therapeutic alliance, which forms the foundation for this trust-building process, is a crucial aspect of therapy. Within this alliance, you find a space where your thoughts and feelings are validated and encouraged to express your deepest emotions without fear of judgment. This safe environment fosters vulnerability, allowing you to explore deep-seated emotional patterns that might remain buried. Through this exploration, you gain insights into how these patterns impact your relationships, empowering you to make conscious changes that enhance your emotional well-being. The therapeutic relationship's sense of safety and understanding creates a powerful catalyst for transformation.

Various therapeutic modalities can aid in transforming attachment styles, each offering unique benefits. Cognitive Behavioral Therapy (CBT) is particularly effective in reframing negative beliefs that may underlie avoidant behaviors. CBT helps you develop healthier thought patterns and behaviors by challenging and reshaping these beliefs. On the other hand, emotionally Focused Therapy (EFT) focuses on enhancing emotional connection, guiding you to express and process emotions in ways that foster intimacy and understanding. Attachment-based therapy offers a more direct approach, addressing specific attachment issues and helping you develop secure relational patterns. These therapies, individually or in combination, provide tailored support to meet your unique needs, guiding you toward healthier and more fulfilling relationships.

Therapy has many benefits for people struggling with avoidant attachment styles. It enhances emotional awareness, enabling you to identify and express your feelings more effectively. Through therapy, you learn to navigate relational interactions with confidence and empathy, building skills that improve your ability to connect with others. The therapeutic process encourages you to confront and embrace your emotions, fostering a sense of emotional resilience. As you become more attuned to your feelings, you gain the tools needed to manage them constructively, reducing the tendency to retreat into emotional distance. This newfound awareness and skill set empower you to engage in healthier, more meaningful relationships, bringing you closer to the secure attachments you desire.

Consistency in therapeutic engagement is vital for achieving meaningful change. Setting a regular therapy schedule ensures you remain committed to the process, providing the stability needed for growth. Consistent sessions allow you to build momentum, progressively working through challenges and celebrating victories. Dedicating to ongoing therapeutic goals reinforces your commitment to personal development, helping you stay focused on the path to transformation. Regular engagement with therapy offers a structured framework for accountability, encouraging you to explore your emotional landscape with intention and purpose. Through this commitment, you cultivate a mindset of continuous growth, embracing the potential for lasting change in your emotional and relational life.

Reflection Section: Therapeutic Engagement Checklist

- **Regular Schedule**: Have you established a consistent therapy schedule?
- **Therapeutic Alliance**: Do you feel safe and understood within the therapeutic relationship?

- **Modality Exploration**: Which therapeutic approaches have you explored, and which resonate with you?
- **Emotional Awareness**: How has therapy helped you recognize and express your emotions?
- **Commitment to Goals**: Are you actively pursuing your therapeutic goals with dedication?

Use this checklist to assess and enhance your therapeutic engagement, ensuring you remain aligned with your personal and relational development objectives.

FINDING THE RIGHT THERAPEUTIC SUPPORT

Choosing a therapist who truly understands your needs is crucial in your path to emotional healing. You are the central figure in this journey, and finding someone specializing in attachment issues can make a significant difference. A therapist with expertise in attachment theory will deeply understand how early relationships affect your current interactions. They can guide you through the complexities of avoidant attachment with insight and empathy. Finding a therapist whose communication style aligns with yours is also vital. Some therapists are more directive, while others take a more collaborative approach. Consider what type of interaction makes you feel most comfortable and empowered. This compatibility can enhance your therapy experience, making it more effective and fulfilling.

The relationship between you and your therapist, often called "therapeutic fit," is crucial to successful therapy. Building rapport and trust with your therapist creates a safe space for exploration and growth. Feeling understood and validated makes you more likely to open up and engage with the process thoroughly. This connection allows you to delve into deeper emotional patterns and work through them with support. A good therapeutic fit fosters a partnership where you and the therapist work together toward your healing goals. This relationship often holds the power to transform your emotional landscape, helping you develop healthier relational patterns.

Evaluating potential therapists can feel overwhelming, but having a strategy can simplify the process. Start with a consultation. It is a good opportunity to ask questions that matter to you. Inquire about their experience with attachment issues and their therapeutic approach. Discuss what you hope to achieve through therapy and gauge their response. This meeting can provide valuable insights into whether the therapist's expertise aligns with your needs. Consider scheduling trial sessions to assess comfort and effectiveness further. These sessions allow you to experience their style firsthand and decide if it feels right. Trust your instincts during this process; feeling at ease is essential to a good match.

In addition to traditional therapy, alternative support options can complement your healing journey. Online therapy platforms offer accessibility and convenience, allowing you to connect with therapists from your home. This can be particularly beneficial if you have a busy schedule or live in an area with limited in-person options. Support groups provide another layer of assistance. They offer a space to share experiences with others who understand what you are going through. These groups can cultivate a sense of community and belonging, providing peer support that can be incredibly validating and empowering. Other alternative options include self-help books, podcasts, and workshops, which can provide additional insights and tools for your healing journey. Engaging with others with similar challenges can broaden your understanding and offer new perspectives on your attachment style.

INTEGRATING BOOK INSIGHTS WITH COUNSELING

Integrating self-help insights with therapy can significantly enhance healing, providing a more holistic approach to personal growth. When you combine the exercises and reflections from this book with your therapeutic sessions, you reinforce the concepts you are working on in therapy. This dual approach can deepen your understanding and help you apply what you learn in real-world settings. The exercises in this book encourage self-reflection, allowing you to internalize therapeutic concepts and explore them more deeply. These exercises can uncover insights that may not arise during therapy sessions alone. This self-guided exploration complements the structured support of therapy, creating a rich framework for personal development.

Discussing the insights and exercises from the book with your therapist can also be incredibly beneficial. It lets you bring personal reflections into your therapy sessions, providing a starting point for deeper discussions. Sharing these reflections helps your therapist understand your thoughts and emotional responses, offering a more comprehensive view of your experiences. Together, you can explore how these insights relate to the issues you are working on in therapy, using them as a springboard for addressing complex topics. Whether it is a specific exercise or a chapter that resonated with you, these elements can facilitate meaningful conversations, helping you to address and resolve underlying challenges. This collaborative approach encourages open dialogue, fostering a partnership between you and your therapist as you work toward shared goals.

To work collaboratively with your therapist using book insights, it can be helpful to set joint goals based on the material. This involves discussing specific objectives you want to achieve and drawing on the concepts and exercises from the book. Your therapist can then tailor their approach to support these goals, providing guidance and feedback that aligns with your personal development plan. Regularly reviewing your progress on book-inspired tasks can help you stay on track and adjust as needed. This ongoing evaluation allows you to measure your growth and celebrate milestones, reinforcing your commitment to the process. You create a dynamic and supportive environment for change by actively engaging with books and therapy resources.

Maintaining a journal to track insights and progress can further enhance your engagement with therapeutic tools. This practice allows you to document your thoughts and experiences, creating a record of your journey. Journaling provides a space for reflection, helping you to process emotions and identify patterns that may influence your behavior. Over weeks and months, these entries can reveal valuable insights, offering a window into your growth and transformation. Creating a personal toolkit from books and therapy resources can also be empowering. This toolkit might include exercises, reflections, and strategies that resonate with you, providing a resource for managing challenges and fostering resilience. By actively using these tools, you enhance your ability to navigate emotional complexities, equipping yourself with the skills to build healthier, more secure relationships.

DEVELOPING A THERAPEUTIC ACTION PLAN

Think about setting out on a road trip without a map or GPS. You know the destination, but each turn and decision requires guesswork, which might lead to unexpected detours. A therapeutic action plan is your roadmap, providing structure and direction as you work toward transforming your attachment patterns. This plan clarifies your therapeutic goals, offering a clear vision of what you wish to achieve. You can see your progress and celebrate each step forward by setting specific milestones. A well-crafted action plan outlines your personal development journey, helping you navigate the complexities of emotional growth with confidence and purpose.

Creating a personalized action plan involves several steps tailored to your unique needs and aspirations. Begin by identifying particular areas where you seek change and growth. Reflect on the patterns and behaviors you wish to alter, considering how they impact your relationships. Once you clearly understand these areas, set realistic timelines for achieving your objectives. Break down your goals into attainable steps, ensuring each milestone is manageable. This process provides a sense of accomplishment and keeps you motivated and focused. You create a cohesive framework to support your emotional and relational development by aligning your plan with your therapeutic goals.

Accountability is crucial to the success of a therapeutic action plan. It ensures you stay committed to your goals, providing the support needed to overcome challenges. Involve your therapist in monitoring your progress, using sessions to discuss achievements and areas for improvement. This collaborative partnership allows you to work together toward common objectives. Additionally, consider enlisting a support partner, someone you trust to hold you accountable. This person can offer encouragement, celebrate successes, and provide perspective when encountering obstacles. Their involvement adds extra support, reinforcing your commitment to personal growth.

To effectively track and evaluate your progress, consider using practical tools that offer clarity and insight. Progress charts and checklists can be valuable resources, allowing you to visualize your achievements and identify areas that require further attention. These tools provide a tangible way to measure your development, offering a sense of direction and purpose. Regular reflection sessions can also enhance your ability to assess progress. Set aside time to evaluate your achievements, reflecting on the steps you have taken and the lessons learned along the way. This practice encourages self-awareness and helps you stay aligned with your goals, ensuring that your action plan remains relevant and practical.

Interactive Element: Action Plan Template

- **Goal Setting**: Define your primary objectives for personal and therapeutic growth.

- **Milestones**: Identify specific milestones that mark progress toward your goals.
- **Timeline**: Create a realistic timeline for reaching each milestone.
- **Accountability**: List your therapist's role and support partner's involvement in monitoring progress.
- **Evaluation Tools**: Choose tools like progress charts and checklists to track development.

Use this template to structure your therapeutic action plan, tailoring it to your needs and aspirations. Review and change your plan regularly as you progress, ensuring it remains a dynamic and supportive resource for your journey toward transformation.

LEVERAGING THERAPY FOR LONG-TERM ATTACHMENT SECURITY

Imagine therapy as a sturdy anchor in the sometimes turbulent sea of life. This anchor does not just stabilize you during storms; it helps you navigate calmer waters as well. The long-term benefits of sustained therapeutic work are profound, reinforcing secure attachment behaviors continuously. Regularly engaging in therapy creates a routine that nurtures emotional growth. This ongoing support helps solidify the new patterns you have worked hard to establish, making them second nature as time passes. As life throws new challenges, therapy acts as a compass, guiding you with strategies and insights tailored to your evolving needs. Whether it is a new job, a relationship shift, or personal growth, therapy provides a framework to adapt and thrive.

The journey does not end when formal therapy sessions conclude. Maintenance strategies become crucial in preserving the progress you have made. Regular self-check-ins and reflections are invaluable tools for staying attuned to your emotional state. Set aside time to reflect on your feelings and behaviors, identifying old patterns that might resurface. Continued practice of therapeutic exercises keeps you grounded, reinforcing the skills you have developed. These exercises, whether mindfulness practices or journaling, remind you of the work you have accomplished and your growth. They act as touchstones, helping you stay connected to your cultivated secure attachment.

Approaching therapy as a lifelong tool rather than a one-time fix changes how you view personal development. Life is dynamic, with transitions and changes that can unsettle even the most secure individuals. Returning to therapy during major life shifts can provide stability and insight to navigate these periods confidently. Periodic therapeutic "tune-ups" offer an opportunity to recalibrate, ensuring that your emotional resilience remains strong. These check-ins with a therapist can prevent regression, letting you address emerging issues before they become overwhelming. This proactive approach to therapy fosters a sense of empowerment, enabling you to take charge of your emotional well-being.

Adopting a mindset focused on lifelong growth and development transforms how you engage with therapy and personal growth. Viewing therapy as part of a more extensive process of self-discovery encourages you to embrace change as an opportunity for continued development. Each therapeutic encounter becomes a stepping stone, contributing to a deeper understanding of yourself and your relationships. This mindset invites you to see challenges as chances to learn and grow, cultivating resilience and adaptability. By embracing this perspective, you open yourself to the richness of life, ready to evolve and thrive in whatever circumstances arise.

In this chapter, we have explored how therapy can serve as a foundation for long-term attachment security. Sustained therapeutic engagement reinforces secure behaviors, helping you adapt to life's ever-changing landscape. Regular self-reflection and proactive therapy ensure lasting growth, turning therapy into a lifelong ally.

CHAPTER 10
FOUNDATIONS OF EMPOWERMENT AND GROWTH IN ATTACHMENT HEALING

THINK OF A SCULPTOR GRADUALLY CHISELING AWAY AT A PROTECTIVE marble shell, each careful stroke revealing the capacity for connection beneath. Just as a sculptor reveals the hidden beauty within the marble, the journey of personal growth and empowerment shapes the inner landscape of who we are. For those of us with avoidant attachment patterns, this shell represents the defensive barriers we have built—our tendency to withdraw, our comfort with emotional distance, and our reflexive self-reliance. Yet beneath these protective layers lies our innate ability to connect. The journey of transforming avoidant attachment requires a delicate balance of self-compassion and courage, acknowledging that our defensive patterns once served a vital purpose while recognizing they may no longer serve our current needs for connection. It takes lots of courage to embark on this journey, face our fears, and step into the unknown, but this courage empowers us.

THE JOURNEY TO SECURE ATTACHMENT

As we have seen, the path from avoidant to secure attachment begins with the understanding that our tendency to withdraw from emotional connection stems from early adaptive responses. Research with avoidant attachment clients reveals that self-compassion often feels threatening precisely because it activates the attachment system we have worked so hard to suppress. One individual, Michael, described his initial resistance to self-compassion practices as follows: "Being kind to myself felt more threatening than criticism. Criticism was familiar; it kept me moving, achieving, staying safe in my independence."

Cultivating self-compassion involves embracing a nonjudgmental attitude toward personal flaws. We are all imperfect, yet it is through these imperfections that we learn and grow. Accepting this truth is liberating, offering the freedom to be human without the burden of unrealistic expectations. When you nurture compassion toward yourself, you create a foundation for genuine self-acceptance. This self-compassion is not a weakness but a source of strength and freedom, empowering you to be your true self and live a life free from the weight of self-criticism.

We can begin with small, manageable steps toward self-compassion to navigate this challenge. Traditional loving-kindness meditation might feel overwhelming for those with avoidant attachment. Instead, start with "micro-moments of compassion." Close your eyes for thirty seconds, focusing on phrases like "My need for space is valid" or "I can be both independent and connected." These brief exercises help bypass our defensive reactions while gradually building tolerance for self-directed warmth.

James, a software engineer with avoidant attachment, developed his "emotional check-in protocol." Each morning, he would spend two minutes acknowledging one emotion and one need without trying to fix or change them. "At first, it felt mechanical, almost like debugging code," he shared. "But over time, it became a way to maintain emotional awareness without feeling overwhelmed."

Integrating self-compassion into daily life is a deliberate practice that requires effort and commitment. Start your day with affirmations reinforcing your worth and capabilities to set a positive tone. Equally important is setting aside time for self-reflection and care. Whether it is a quiet walk in nature or a few minutes of mindful breathing, these practices ground you in the present and nurture your well-being, fostering a compassionate outlook on life.

Interactive Element: Self-Compassion Checklist

- **Morning Affirmations**: Begin each day by affirming your worth and setting a positive intention.
- **Loving-Kindness Meditation**: Practice visualizing compassion and kindness for yourself and others.
- **Mindful Breathing**: Set aside time for deep breaths, grounding yourself in the present moment.
- **Reflective Journaling**: Write about daily experiences, focusing on self-kindness and understanding.

These practices cultivate an enduring sense of self-compassion, bringing about profound personal growth. By embracing this approach, you empower yourself to face life's challenges with resilience and grace, creating a life imbued with authenticity and joy.

EMPOWERMENT THROUGH KNOWLEDGE AND AWARENESS

For those with avoidant attachment, intellectual understanding often feels safer than emotional connection. This preference for knowledge can be used as a bridge toward greater emotional awareness. Dr. Mark Thompson's research on attachment styles shows that avoidant individuals often begin their healing journey through intellectual engagement before developing emotional capacity. Consider creating what Dr. Thompson calls an "attachment insight journal." Each week, record the following:

1. One attachment pattern you noticed.
2. The situation that triggered it.
3. Your bodily sensations during activation.
4. The emotional need beneath the pattern.
5. One small way you might respond differently next time.

A research scientist, Louise, found that approaching her attachment patterns with scientific curiosity helped reduce shame and increase awareness. "I started treating my attachment responses like data points in a longitudinal study," she explained. "This created enough emotional distance to observe my patterns without immediately withdrawing from them."

Increasing self-awareness is a key to personal empowerment. It guides us through the complex emotional landscapes of our lives. Understanding attachment theory gives us valuable insights into how early experiences shape our behaviors. It empowers us to make informed choices about our relationships. It is like a lighthouse, illuminating the path and helping us navigate troubled emotional waters.

Again, mindfulness meditation practices offer another structured way to cultivate this awareness. Traditional meditation might feel overwhelming for those with avoidant attachment, so start with brief moments of conscious attention. Set aside just two minutes daily to direct your attention to your breath and notice your thoughts with nonjudgmental awareness. This creates a safe space for self-reflection and insight while respecting your need for emotional regulation.

STRATEGIES FOR SUSTAINABLE PERSONAL CHANGE

For those with avoidant attachment, sustainable change requires balancing our need for independence with our growing capacity for connection. This balance begins with recognizing that independence and connection can coexist—they are not mutually exclusive states. Maya, a freelance designer, developed what she called her "connection capacity building" practice:

1. **Morning**: Brief emotional check-in (two minutes)

- Name one emotion
- Identify one relationship need

- Set one small connection intention for the day

2. **Throughout the Day**: Micro-connections

- Send one authentic message to a friend
- Share a genuine observation with a colleague
- Practice thirty seconds of eye contact in conversations

3. **Evening**: Integration practice (five minutes)

- Review moments of connection and withdrawal
- Acknowledge both independence and connection needs
- Plan the next day's balance points

For maintaining long-term change, Dr. James Wilson's research identifies key sustainability factors for those with avoidant attachment:

1. **Structure and Flexibility**: Create consistent connection practices while allowing for adaptation during high-stress periods. Rather than seeing withdrawal as a failure, plan for it: *If I need to withdraw, I'll communicate it and set a specific time to reconnect.*
2. **Progressive Challenge**: Gradually increase emotional exposure while maintaining successful experiences. Start with written communication, progress to voice calls, and then face-to-face vulnerability.
3. **Independence Integration**: Integrate both needs rather than viewing independence as an opposing connection.

Schedule both connection time and explicit alone time, honoring both as valuable.

Remember that sustainable change is like a steady drumbeat—consistent and enduring rather than a sprint followed by exhaustion. This is particularly important for those with avoidant attachment, who might be tempted to approach emotional growth with the same intensity they bring to achievement-oriented goals. Here are some common challenges and solutions:

1. **Achievement-Based Regression**:

- **Challenge**: Returning to achievement focus during stress
- **Solution**: Create "connection metrics" alongside traditional goals

2. **Withdrawal Impulse**:

- **Challenge**: Strong urges to disconnect during intimacy
- **Solution**: Develop "partial withdrawal" strategies that maintain some connection

3. **Emotional Overwhelm**:

- **Challenge**: Feeling flooded when practicing connection
- **Solution**: Create emotional "container times" with clear start and endpoints

Dr. Wilson notes, "Sustainable change for those with avoidant attachment isn't about eliminating the avoidant response but expanding our capacity to choose connection even when avoidance feels safer." Remember, transforming avoidant attachment patterns is not about becoming a different person—it is about expanding your capacity for connection while honoring your need for independence. Each small step toward secure attachment builds upon the last, creating lasting change through consistent, mindful practice. The journey requires patience, self-compassion, and the understanding that growth happens gradually, one conscious choice at a time.

CHAPTER 11
TOOLS FOR TRANSFORMATION

THIS CHAPTER WILL EXPLORE THE TOOLS YOU NEED FOR YOUR transformative journey of understanding and redefining your attachment styles. You are at the center of this journey, and your active participation is crucial. Journaling for self-reflection can uncover deep insights that foster personal growth. At the same time, reflective questions will guide you in examining your relationship patterns, allowing you to understand how your past influences your present. We will introduce practical attachment exercises that can be seamlessly integrated into everyday life, helping to reinforce healthier responses in your interactions. We will also outline how to create a personalized attachment change plan, equipping you with the tools to navigate your unique path toward healthier attachments. Finally, building a supportive community, whether it is through therapy, support groups, or trusted friends, will be crucial in this process, as sharing experiences offers perspective and encouragement. These elements will lay the foundation for meaningful change and personal development, with you as the central figure in this journey.

COMPREHENSIVE JOURNALING PRACTICE

Consider journaling as a robust tool for self-reflection and personal growth. Just as a painter uses strokes to bring their vision to life, you can use words to paint the landscape of your inner world. This practice is more than just putting pen to paper; it is a journey that explores your thoughts, emotions, and experiences in a safe space. Through consistent journaling, you can process emotions, confront fears, celebrate victories, and develop clarity about your attachment style. Writing helps structure your internal dialogue, transforming abstract feelings into tangible insights that enhance self-awareness and emotional regulation. By examining how past experiences influence present relationships through written expression, you gain profound perspectives that guide your growth journey.

To assist in this exploration, consider incorporating a variety of journaling prompts into your practice. These prompts are designed to guide you in examining different facets of your attachment style and relationships. Start by reflecting on past relationship experiences. What were the dynamics like? How did you feel during moments of closeness or conflict? Another prompt might invite you to explore your current emotional triggers and responses. When do you feel the urge to withdraw, and what emotions arise in those moments? Understanding these triggers can empower you to navigate your feelings more effectively.

Additionally, consider writing about a time you felt deeply connected to someone. What factors contributed to that connection, and how can you cultivate similar experiences now? These prompts encourage introspection, helping you uncover insights that might otherwise remain hidden.

Making journaling a regular part of your routine helps maximize its positive impact on your life. Incorporate this practice into your routine to foster ongoing self-exploration. You should journal daily, taking a few moments each morning or evening to jot down your thoughts. Alternatively, a weekly journaling session can provide a dedicated space for deeper reflection. Set up a comfortable and quiet area where you can write undisturbed. This dedicated space signals to your mind that it is time to focus inward, creating a ritual supporting your self-discovery journey. Eventually, this practice becomes a valuable tool for maintaining self-awareness and emotional balance.

Reviewing past journal entries is an enlightening exercise that allows you to track emotional and behavioral changes over weeks, months, and years. As you read through your entries, you may notice recurring themes or patterns, such as a tendency to avoid intimacy during stressful periods. Identifying these patterns can inform your relationship approach, highlighting areas where growth is needed. Additionally, revisiting your entries can provide a sense of progress, reminding you how far you have come on your journey toward secure attachment. This sense of progress can instill a feeling of accomplishment, motivating you to continue building on your strengths and address challenges confidently and clearly.

Interactive Element: Journaling Prompts for Self-Exploration

- Reflect on a past relationship where you felt emotionally distant. What factors contributed to this distance, and how did it affect the relationship?
- Explore a recent situation that triggered a strong emotional response. What were you feeling, and what thoughts accompanied those feelings?
- Write about a time when you felt deeply connected to someone. What elements fostered that connection, and how can you bring similar qualities into current relationships?
- Consider a pattern you have noticed in your relationships. How does this pattern relate to your attachment style, and what steps can you take to address it?

As you engage with these prompts, allow yourself the freedom to explore without judgment. Journaling can support your development and understanding and provide a window into your inner world.

Reflective Questions for Deeper Learning

Reflective questioning illuminates the path to deeper self-understanding by encouraging critical thinking and introspection. These questions serve as mirrors, reflecting aspects of yourself that may remain unexplored, facilitating both personal and relational insights. Through this process, you uncover the underlying beliefs and values guiding your behaviors while gaining clarity about complex emotions and thoughts. Start by examining your values and relationship goals through targeted questions about vulnerability, trust, and partnership dynamics. Consider how your past influences your present ability to connect and what principles matter most in your relationships. This focused exploration offers a richer understanding of the factors shaping your interactions.

While these questions provide a starting point, I encourage you to create a personalized set of questions. Your unique experiences and challenges are the keys to unlocking a more profound understanding. Reflect on areas of curiosity or uncertainty in your life. There may be a recurring issue in your relationships that you cannot quite figure out. Formulate questions that address these specific dynamics. For example, if you often struggle with expressing emotions, you might ask, "What fears hold me from sharing my true feelings?" Tailoring questions in this way allows you to address the nuances of your experiences, leading to more targeted and meaningful introspection. This personalized approach ensures that your reflection is profoundly relevant and impactful, guiding you toward greater clarity and growth.

Once again, discussion also plays a vital role in the process of reflection. Conversations with trusted friends or partners about your reflective questions can enhance understanding and provide new perspectives. Sharing your insights and hearing others' viewpoints can deepen your comprehension of complex issues. It fosters a collaborative environment where mutual learning and support thrive. Consider participating in group discussions or workshops focused on personal growth. These settings offer a safe space to explore complex topics, allowing you to learn from others' experiences and gain diverse insights. The collective wisdom of a group can illuminate blind spots and broaden your perspective, enriching your reflective practice. Whether in intimate conversations or larger gatherings, discussing your reflections with others can amplify their impact, leading to profound personal and relational transformation.

Reflection plays a pivotal role in sustaining change, acting as a mirror that allows you to see your growth and adjust your course as needed. In the context of personal development, regular reflection sessions offer an opportunity to assess your progress, celebrate successes, and identify areas for improvement. It helps you stay connected with your journey, fostering greater self-awareness and emotional intelligence. In relationships, reflection can provide valuable insights into your partner's needs and feelings, promoting empathy and understanding. Consider keeping a reflective journal to document your thoughts, feelings, and experiences. This journal becomes a living record of your transformation, providing a tangible way to measure your progress and maintain momentum.

Interactive Element: Reflective Journal Prompts

- What new behaviors have you successfully integrated into your daily life?
- How have these changes impacted your relationships?
- What challenges have you encountered, and how have you overcome them?
- In what ways have you noticed growth in your emotional awareness?

PERSONALIZED GROWTH PLANNING AND GOAL SETTING

A tailored change plan is your transformation guide, providing structure and clarity while reflecting your unique strengths and challenges. You create a realistic roadmap that transforms abstract desires into tangible goals by aligning strategies with your traits and setting clear, achievable objectives. These objectives should stretch you just enough to encourage growth without overwhelming you, becoming milestones that build confidence and momentum. Begin by identifying and breaking specific attachment-related goals into manageable steps with realistic timelines. For instance, if improving communication is your goal, practice active listening daily. This systematic approach ensures steady progress while maintaining focus and accountability.

Setting Personal Growth Goals

For those with avoidant attachment patterns, goal setting often gravitates toward achievement rather than connection. We might feel more comfortable setting career advancement or skill development goals than emotional vulnerability. While these achievement-oriented goals have value, healing avoidant attachment requires us to expand our focus to include relationship-oriented goals.

Consider Rachelle's experience as a successful attorney. She excelled at setting and achieving professional goals. However, she initially resisted when her therapist suggested setting goals around the emotional connection. "I could plan a complex litigation strategy, but planning to be more vulnerable felt foreign and frightening." This resistance reflects how our attachment patterns can influence our personal development approach. Together, they developed what they called "balanced growth goals," pairing each achievement goal with a connection goal:

- **Achievement Goal #1**: Complete advanced certification in legal mediation
- **Connection Goal #1**: Share one personal feeling during each weekly team meeting
- **Achievement Goal #2**: Improve time management efficiency
- **Connection Goal #2**: Spend ten minutes in unstructured conversation with her partner daily

When creating these types of goals, you can use the SMART (specific, measurable, achievable, relevant, time-bound) framework while acknowledging attachment activation:

1. **Specific**: Instead of "be more open," try "share one vulnerability with my closest friend each week."
2. **Measurable**: Track the action and your attachment response (e.g., Did you feel the urge to withdraw?).
3. **Achievable**: Start small to manage attachment anxiety.
4. **Relevant**: Connect goals to your desire for secure attachment.
5. **Time-bound**: Set realistic timeframes that account for attachment challenges.

Just as standing at the edge of a vast field can feel overwhelming without a clear path, setting personal growth goals provides direction and focus for your healing journey. These goals serve as guideposts, helping you channel your efforts toward meaningful change while respecting your attachment-based needs for safety and control.

Tracking and evaluating your progress is vital in achieving personal growth goals. Keeping a personal growth journal can be an invaluable tool in this process. Dedicate weekly time to reflect on your progress, noting successes and challenges. This practice allows you to celebrate achievements and identify areas for improvement. Regularly reviewing your goals ensures they remain aligned with your evolving priorities, enabling you to adjust them as needed. Perhaps you realize that a goal is irrelevant or that you have accomplished more than anticipated. By revisiting your goals, you can make informed decisions about how to proceed, ensuring your growth efforts remain focused and effective.

Celebrating milestones and achievements is essential to maintaining motivation and reinforcing progress. Create a rewards system to acknowledge your accomplishments, no matter how small. When you reach a milestone, treat yourself to a special meal or a relaxing day off. These rewards serve as positive reinforcements, encouraging continued effort and dedication. Reflecting on growth and lessons learned is equally essential. Consider what you have gained from the process regarding achievements and insights. This reflection helps solidify your progress, embedding the changes you have made into your life. It also provides an opportunity to learn from setbacks, equipping you with the knowledge to navigate future challenges. As you celebrate your growth, remember that each step takes you closer to realizing your full potential.

Flexibility is crucial in planning, as life rarely unfolds exactly as expected. Your plan should be a living document, open to adjustments based on feedback and progress. Embrace new insights as they arise, allowing them to inform your path forward. This adaptability prevents stagnation, ensuring that your plan remains relevant and practical. As you progress, you might discover areas that require more attention or find that specific steps need reevaluation. By remaining open to evolution, you cultivate resilience and foster continuous growth. This willingness to adapt enhances your plan and strengthens your capacity to navigate life's uncertainties gracefully and confidently.

Monitoring and evaluating your plan is an ongoing process that keeps you aligned with your goals. Progress journals or digital apps can be invaluable tools for tracking your journey. Regularly record your achievements, setbacks, and reflections to gain insights into your progress. These records help you identify patterns, celebrate successes, and swiftly address challenges. Set aside time periodically to assess and revise your strategy, ensuring it evolves with your growth. During these reviews, ask yourself what has worked well and needs adjustment. This reflective practice reinforces accountability and keeps your efforts focused and intentional. It also provides a sense of accomplishment, reminding you how far you have come.

USE HEALTHY ATTACHMENT EXERCISES DAILY

Incorporating practical exercises into your daily routine can significantly reinforce your work on attachment, making the abstract tangible and the theoretical-practical. Imagine the satisfaction of having simple tools at your disposal, ready to be used whenever emotional regulation or relational skills need a boost. Here, we will briefly review valuable attachment exercises to practice daily.

Among these tools we have stressed are mindfulness practices designed to help you manage emotions effectively. One such practice is mindful breathing, where you focus on the rhythm of your breath to find calmness amid chaos. This exercise can be done anywhere, offering a refuge from the stress and an opportunity to center yourself. Another valuable exercise is a body scan meditation, which requires checking different areas of your body to notice where you are. Holding stress and consciously releasing it are simple mindfulness practices that are incredibly effective in helping you stay grounded.

As explored earlier in the book, communication exercises are also pivotal in enhancing your relational skills. Consider the practice of active listening, which involves genuinely paying attention to what others are saying without planning your response. This exercise can transform conversations, allowing for deeper understanding and connection. Another exercise is using "I" statements, which help you express feelings without blaming others. For instance, instead of saying, "You never listen to me," you might say, "I feel unheard when my thoughts are not acknowledged." These exercises encourage openness and honesty, fostering meaningful dialogues and reducing misunderstandings.

Variety is the spice of life, and the same applies to the exercises you choose to integrate into your routine. For those looking to build trust and openness, consider exercises like sharing daily reflections with a partner, trusted family member, or friend. This technique requires dedicating a specific period daily to share one thing you appreciate about each other, reinforcing positivity and connection. To foster emotional intimacy, you might engage in an activity called "emotional check-ins," where you regularly discuss your emotional state with others, identifying feelings and exploring their origins. These exercises cater to different needs and help strengthen the bonds of trust and intimacy in your relationships.

Finding Consistency Through Structure and Adaptation

Imagine you are on a scenic hike, winding through a lush, ever-changing landscape. The path is unclear, but each step brings you closer to your destination. This hike is akin to the journey of sustaining attachment transformation. It is one thing to start this process, but maintaining it requires dedication and a strategy to integrate new patterns into your everyday life. Consistency becomes your steady companion, providing stability needed to reinforce new habits and avoid slipping back into old patterns. Consistency sets the stage for long-term success by anchoring your progress in reliable, repeatable actions. It forms the foundation upon which transformation can thrive, ensuring that each new behavior becomes a natural part of your daily existence.

Consistency is not merely about repetition; it is about creating a sense of stability and predictability in your life. As emphasized in behavior support strategies, consistency aids in setting clear expectations and enhances self-esteem by providing a dependable framework for growth. By reinforcing new habits regularly, you build a strong foundation that supports emotional regulation and resilience. This reliability helps prevent complacency, which can be a silent adversary on your path to change. It is easy to fall back into comfortable but unproductive habits without consistent reinforcement. Consider consistency as the gentle yet persistent waves shaping the shore, gradually transforming the landscape over a lifetime. It is through this steady application that true, lasting transformation occurs.

Consider creating a structure that naturally incorporates attachment exercises to embed transformation into your daily routine. This might involve starting your day with a brief mindfulness practice, such as a five-minute meditation, or ending it with reflective journaling, where you write down three things you are grateful for. These small, deliberate actions can solidify new patterns and make them second nature. Utilizing technology can also be advantageous; apps and reminders can serve as gentle nudges, keeping you on track. For instance, setting reminders to practice gratitude or checking in with your emotions can help integrate these practices into your daily rhythm. The key is to weave these activities seamlessly into your life so they become as habitual as brushing your teeth. These practices will reinforce your progress and enrich your overall well-being as days pass.

Consistency is crucial for lasting change, so weaving these exercises into your daily life is essential. Setting reminders can help ensure that these practices become part of your routine. Whether it is a gentle nudge on your phone reminding you to take a mindful breath or an alarm signaling a time for an emotional check-in, these reminders keep you accountable. Integrate these exercises into existing routines, like practicing mindful breathing during your morning coffee or using "I" statements in your evening conversations. These small, consistent actions add up as days pass, gradually transforming your relational landscape.

Adapting exercises to suit your unique context is also key to making them effective. You should tailor these practices to fit your individual or relationship needs. For example, consider doing mindfulness exercises during lunch breaks if you find morning routines challenging. Adjust the intensity or frequency based on your progress and comfort level. If daily emotional check-ins feel overwhelming, start once a week. You can start with meetings and increase the frequency as you gain confidence. Remember, these exercises are meant to support your growth, so feel free to modify them to serve you best.

BUILDING A SUPPORTIVE COMMUNITY

Visualize standing on the edge of a vast ocean, waves crashing against the shore. While this scene might evoke feelings of solitude, the vastness becomes less daunting when surrounded by a supportive community. This network provides essential emotional support, diverse perspectives, and shared experiences that enrich your understanding of yourself and your relationships. Within this community, you find people who empathize with your challenges and celebrate your triumphs, offering insights you might not have considered alone.

Begin building this network by identifying supportive individuals in your life and considering both in-person and virtual connections through support groups or online forums. These varied channels create a comprehensive support system that adapts to your comfort level and schedule while consistently encouraging your attachment work. Also, joining online forums or social media groups focused on attachment work can expand your network beyond geographical boundaries. These platforms connect you with a worldwide community of individuals on similar paths, offering diverse insights and experiences. The digital space allows for flexible participation, enabling you to engage according to your schedule and comfort level.

Diversity and inclusivity within your support network are crucial for enriched learning and growth. Welcoming members from different backgrounds and experiences broaden the range of perspectives and insights available to the group. Diverse voices contribute to a richer tapestry of understanding, offering unique viewpoints that challenge assumptions and expand horizons. Celebrating this diversity means valuing each person's contribution and recognizing the strength that comes from many experiences. It creates an inclusive environment where all members feel seen, heard, and respected. This inclusivity fosters an atmosphere of openness and trust, where people can express themselves authentically without fear of judgment. In such a community, learning becomes a shared journey where each member benefits from the collective wisdom and support of the group.

One of the essential benefits of a supportive community is the mutual accountability it fosters. Accountability partners within your network can help maintain progress and motivation by setting shared goals and regular check-ins. These partners serve as cheerleaders and challengers, supporting your achievements while encouraging you to push beyond your comfort zone. Collaborative problem-solving within the community can lead to innovative solutions and more profound understanding as different perspectives are shared and considered. Peer feedback offers fresh insights into your attachment work, highlighting areas for growth and celebration. This mutual support and accountability environment creates a dynamic where progress is celebrated, and setbacks are viewed as opportunities for learning and development.

Sustaining Growth Through Support Systems

Adequate support systems are essential for long-term success in transforming attachment patterns. These support structures include professional guidance when needed, community resources, and peer support networks. They provide the foundation necessary for maintaining positive changes over time:

1. **Monitoring Progress**: Regularly assessing attachment patterns and relationship dynamics helps maintain positive changes. This involves staying attuned to family interactions, addressing challenges, and celebrating progress. Families can strengthen attachment bonds through consistent monitoring and adjustment and create lasting positive change.

2. **Building Resilience**: The ultimate goal in transforming attachment patterns is building resilience that can weather life's challenges. This involves developing adaptive coping mechanisms, maintaining healthy boundaries, and fostering open communication channels. As families develop these skills, they create a legacy of secure attachment that can benefit future generations.

Support and guidance from others can be invaluable in maintaining your transformation. Engaging with therapists, mentors, or peer groups provides a network of accountability and encouragement. Therapists can offer professional insights and strategies tailored to your unique needs, mentors can provide guidance based on their own experiences, and peer groups can offer shared experiences and mutual support. Scheduled periodic check-ins with a therapist or coach can guide you through challenges and strengthen your commitment to change. These professionals provide insights and strategies tailored to your unique needs, enhancing your capacity for growth.

Additionally, joining support networks or groups can create a sense of community where shared experiences and mutual support foster resilience. Within these communities, you can share your challenges and triumphs, learn from others' experiences, and receive encouragement and advice. These connections can inspire and motivate you, offering fresh perspectives and collective wisdom. They remind you that you are not alone and can achieve remarkable transformation together. This sense of community can make you feel understood and supported, strengthening your resolve to continue your personal growth and relationship improvement journey.

As this chapter draws to a close, consider the power of having a personalized attachment change plan. By tailoring your approach, you harness your strengths, address your challenges, and set a course for meaningful transformation. These structured steps pave the way for secure, fulfilling relationships, building a future where connection and growth thrive. With this plan in hand, you are equipped to embark on a journey of self-discovery and relational enrichment. Embrace the possibilities, and be confident in creating lasting change and meaningful connections.

CHAPTER 12
LEGACY AND LONG-TERM GROWTH

THIS FINAL CHAPTER WILL EXPLORE HOW TO BUILD SECURE AND meaningful relationships by creating a clear vision for the future. By identifying our core values and setting specific goals, we can navigate our journeys together with intention and purpose. We will discuss the importance of aligning our daily actions with this vision, fostering mutual support, and maintaining a positive mindset. Embracing lifelong learning and collaboration will empower us to strengthen our bonds and overcome challenges, ultimately guiding us toward fulfilling and resilient relationships.

CREATING YOUR VISION FOR SECURE RELATIONSHIPS

Envisioning your future in relationships is like charting a course for an adventurous trip. It is about setting a clear direction that aligns with your deepest values and aspirations, giving you a sense of purpose and focus. Defining the core values that you hold dear is the first step in crafting this vision. These values may include honesty, loyalty, or empathy—principles that guide your interactions and decisions. Reflect on what is essential to you in a relationship, and let these values shape your vision. They act as a compass, steering you toward relationships that reflect these ideals. Alongside these values, setting long-term relational goals helps lay the groundwork for a fulfilling future. These goals involve building a family, traveling together, or cultivating a shared passion. They are the milestones that mark your journey, providing motivation and excitement as you move forward.

Everyday actions are the building blocks of your long-term vision. It is vital to align these actions with the future you aspire to create. Begin by regularly revisiting and refining your vision statement. This process ensures that your goals remain relevant and inspiring as you grow and change. It is an opportunity to reflect on what is working and what might need adjustment. Think of your vision statement as a living document that evolves with you. Aligning daily choices with this vision involves making intentional decisions that support your goals. Whether spending quality time with your partner, family members, or friends, prioritizing communication, or investing in shared experiences, each choice contributes to realizing your vision. Though seemingly small, these actions accumulate over months and years, bringing your long-term goals within reach. They keep you grounded and focused, ensuring your daily life reflects your aspirations. This alignment with your long-term vision gives your daily actions a sense of purpose and commitment, bringing your goals within reach.

Mutual support is the cornerstone of achieving any long-term vision. It requires collaboration and shared effort, where both people are invested in the journey. Creating a partnership agreement can be a powerful tool in this endeavor. This agreement outlines shared objectives and commitments, such as regular date nights, open communication, or mutual respect, ensuring that both parties are aligned in pursuing the vision. It reminds you of the goals you have set together, fostering accountability and mutual support. Regular vision-alignment discussions further reinforce this collaboration. These conversations provide open dialogue where partners can express their hopes, concerns, and ideas. They help maintain clarity and focus, ensuring that both individuals are on the same page. This mutual support creates a sense of unity, where challenges are faced, and successes are shared. It strengthens the bond, making the relationship more resilient and fulfilling.

Maintaining hope and optimism is crucial for staying motivated and inspired. It is cultivating a positive outlook, even in the face of challenges. Practicing gratitude and appreciation in your relationships is a powerful tool to develop this mindset. Consistently recognizing the positive qualities of your relationship and expressing gratitude for the other person's presence reinforces your bond. It shifts the focus from what is lacking to what is abundant, creating an atmosphere of positivity and appreciation. This focus on gratitude helps you maintain a positive and appreciative mindset, even in the face of challenges, keeping your vision alive and your commitment strong.

Future Growth and Relationship Empowerment

In the ever-evolving landscape of personal growth and relationships, the mindset of lifelong learning becomes crucial. Imagine your journey as a tapestry, with each new experience adding a vibrant thread. Viewing challenges not as barriers but as chances for expansion allows you to weave a rich and diverse pattern. Every experience, whether a success or a setback, contributes to personal and relational development. This mindset encourages seeking new learning opportunities, such as workshops or classes, which can introduce fresh perspectives and skills. These experiences equip you with tools to navigate the complexities of relationships, enhancing personal satisfaction and relational harmony. By viewing growth as a continuous process, you remain open to change and learning, which can lead to profound transformations in how you connect with yourself and others.

Empowering relationships involves nurturing both individual and collective growth. It means creating a relationship where both partners feel empowered to be their best selves and support each other's growth. One practical approach is joint goal setting with your partner or family members. This process involves agreeing on common personal development objectives, relationship milestones, or shared dreams. By aligning your goals, you create a sense of partnership and shared purpose that strengthens your bond. Collaborative decision-making further empowers your relationship, creating a space where both perspectives are acknowledged and valued. This approach builds trust and mutual respect as decisions reflect both people's collective wisdom and desires. Regularly practicing these skills develops a cooperative dynamic where challenges are met with united effort and successes are celebrated. This empowerment enriches your relationship, allowing it to flourish as people grow individually and together.

Adaptability stands as a cornerstone in navigating the inevitable changes that life presents. The ability to remain flexible in the face of shifting dynamics is invaluable. It enables you to embrace change gracefully, turning potential disruptions into opportunities for growth. This adaptability involves developing strategies to manage unexpected challenges, such as changes in circumstances or evolving needs within the relationship. By cultivating resilience, you equip yourself to respond to these changes confidently and creatively. This mindset supports maintaining balance and harmony, even when faced with uncertainty. Embracing flexibility in relationship dynamics also means being open to adjusting roles and responsibilities as needed, reflecting the fluid nature of healthy partnerships. This adaptability fosters a sense of security and stability, as both people trust in their ability to navigate life's twists and turns together. It reassures you that you can handle whatever life throws your way, strengthening your sense of security and stability in your relationships.

Creating a culture of growth within your relationship involves fostering an environment where mutual empowerment and development are priorities. Celebrating shared successes and progress reinforces the positive aspects of your relationship, creating a strong foundation for future growth. These celebrations, whether big or small, recognize the efforts and achievements of both people, building a sense of accomplishment and motivation.

Encouraging open dialogue about personal growth aspirations further strengthens your connection, allowing each person to express their dreams and goals. This openness fosters understanding and support, creating a safe space where both people feel valued and encouraged to pursue their aspirations. This culture of growth transforms your relationship into a supportive ecosystem where each partner's growth is celebrated and nurtured. The synergy created by this mutual support enhances the overall quality of the relationship, enriching both individual lives and the shared journey.

As you journey through this chapter, remember that creating a long-term vision for your relationships is dynamic. It is about dreaming boldly, planning strategically, and acting consistently. It demands bravery and dedication, yet the rewards are profound. A clear vision guides your actions and enriches your relationships, making them more meaningful and satisfying. As you look forward to the next chapter, know that this vision is a foundation for building stronger, more secure connections. Let it inspire you and lead you to the fulfilling relational life you seek.

BREAKING THE CYCLE OF ATTACHMENT DISSATISFACTION

Reflect on your relationships, both past and present. You may notice a familiar pattern, a cycle of dissatisfaction that seems to replay with each new partner. These recurring patterns often stem from attachment styles established early in life, repeating themselves in a loop that feels inescapable. Perhaps you find yourself constantly seeking reassurance yet never feeling genuinely secure. Or maybe you maintain emotional distance, fearing the vulnerability that closeness demands. The emotional toll of this cycle can be exhausting, leaving you feeling unfulfilled and disconnected. Recognizing these patterns not as a fault but as a starting point for change is essential. Understanding them allows you to see your relationships with fresh eyes, acknowledging how they have impacted your happiness and well-being.

The cycle of avoidant attachment often manifests as a predictable pattern. As relationships deepen, we feel an increasing urge to withdraw, creating an emotional distance that confirms our belief that the connection is threatening. Dr. Elena Martinez's research identifies key phases in this cycle:

1. **Initial Engagement**: We may appear open and connected while maintaining internal distance.
2. **Activation Point**: As emotional intimacy increases, our attachment system activates.
3. **Withdrawal Phase**: We create distance through work, hobbies, or emotional shutdown.
4. **Confirmation Phase**: The resulting relationship strain reinforces our avoidant patterns.

Consider Tim's experience breaking this cycle: "I used to pride myself on being 'low maintenance' in relationships, not needing much contact or emotional connection. When my partner expressed hurt about my emotional distance, I'd withdraw further, seeing their need for connection as proof that closeness was overwhelming." Through therapy, Tim learned to recognize his withdrawal as a protective response rather than a personality trait.

To disrupt these patterns, we can implement what Dr. Sarah Martinez calls "conscious connection practices":

1. **Withdrawal Recognition**:

- Track situations that trigger your urge to withdraw.
- Notice physical sensations that precede emotional disconnection.
- Identify thought patterns that justify distance.

2. **Active Engagement Strategies**:

- When noticing withdrawal urges, practice staying present for just five minutes longer.
- Share your withdrawal process with trusted others: "I'm feeling the urge to pull away right now."
- Create structured connection points that feel manageable.

Dr. Sarah Chen's work with avoidant clients emphasizes the importance of "titrated exposure" to emotional connection. "Think of it like building physical endurance," she explains. "You wouldn't run a marathon without training. Similarly, we build emotional connection capacity gradually."

Understanding and Breaking Intergenerational Patterns

In previous chapters, we delved deeply into understanding avoidant attachment and the effects of childhood wounds, personal triggers, and the development of emotional intimacy. As we move forward, we must explore how to break intergenerational patterns that perpetuate avoidant attachment styles, creating a ripple effect across relationships and families.

At the heart of attachment work lies the crucial task of understanding how family history shapes our present relationships. Families carry forward genetic traits and emotional patterns that influence how we connect with others. These patterns often stretch back multiple generations, creating intricate webs of behavioral and emotional responses that become deeply embedded in family dynamics. Examining these historical threads, we can understand why certain attachment styles persist and how they influence current relationships.

1. **Cultural and Environmental Factors**: Family attachment patterns do not exist independently but are profoundly shaped by cultural, social, and historical contexts. Significant events like wars, economic hardships, or migrations can dramatically shape how families relate to one another across generations. These external factors often imprint on family systems, affecting everything from parenting styles to emotional expression. Understanding these contextual elements helps explain why specific patterns emerged and persisted within family lines.

2. **Identifying Pattern Recognition**: Recognizing attachment patterns requires careful observation and reflection. Family members often unconsciously replicate relationship dynamics experienced in childhood, perpetuating cycles that may span generations. These

patterns manifest in daily interactions, emotional responses, and approaches to conflict resolution. By developing awareness of these recurring themes, individuals can identify which patterns serve them well and which ones may need transformation.

Breaking the Cycle of Trauma: Understanding Trauma's Ripple Effect

Generational trauma operates like invisible threads connecting past experiences to present behaviors. This form of inherited trauma can manifest in various ways, from explicit fears and anxieties to subtle patterns of emotional withdrawal or overprotection. The impact of unresolved trauma often appears in how family members relate to one another, make decisions, and handle stress. Recognizing these patterns is essential for beginning the healing process.

1. **The Path to Healing**: Healing from generational trauma requires both individual and collective work within family systems. This journey involves acknowledging past wounds while developing new coping mechanisms and relationship patterns. Professional support often plays an essential role in this process, offering tools and perspectives to help family members process their experiences and develop healthier ways of relating to one another.
2. **Creating New Patterns**: Transforming trauma patterns begins with conscious awareness and intentional action. This includes developing new communication styles,

establishing healthy boundaries, and learning to respond rather than react to emotional triggers. Through consistent practice and support, families can gradually replace harmful patterns with nurturing ones that promote healing and growth.

CREATING YOUR SECURE ATTACHMENT LEGACY

Creating a secure attachment legacy starts with understanding the essential elements contributing to emotional safety and trust. These include consistent emotional availability, reliable responses to needs, and the ability to repair relationship ruptures. These fundamental components form the building blocks for developing more substantial, resilient family bonds:

1. **Implementation Strategies**: Transforming attachment patterns requires practical strategies that can be implemented in daily life. This includes establishing regular family connection times, developing emotional coaching skills, and creating environments that support open communication. Success often comes through small, consistent actions rather than dramatic changes.

2. **Future-Focused Development**: Supporting secure attachment in future generations involves ongoing education and skill development. Parents and caregivers benefit from understanding attachment theory and its practical applications. This knowledge, combined with emotional regulation techniques and communication skills, helps create an environment where secure attachment can flourish.

Creating a secure attachment legacy involves fostering deep, meaningful relationships that cultivate trust, understanding, and emotional safety. At the core of this process is recognizing how our attachment styles shape interactions and connections with others. Here are some key steps toward establishing a legacy of secure attachments:

1. **Understanding Attachment Styles**: Begin by exploring your attachment style—secure, anxious, avoidant, or disorganized. Understanding your patterns can help you recognize how they influence your relationships and provide insight into how to nurture healthier connections.

2. **Modeling Secure Attachments**: Be intentional about demonstrating trustworthy and reliable behaviors. Show consistency in your words and actions; this builds a foundation of security for those around you. Share your feelings openly and encourage others to do the same, creating a safe emotional space.

3. **Practicing Active Listening**: Make it a habit to listen to others, genuinely validating their feelings and perspectives. This strengthens bonds and reinforces feelings of safety and belonging, essential elements of secure attachments.

4. **Encouraging Vulnerability**: Creating an environment where vulnerability is welcomed is vital. Share your experiences and struggles, showing that expressing emotions and seeking support is okay. This reciprocal openness fosters a deeper connection.

5. **Conflict Resolution**: Embrace healthy conflict resolution techniques. When disagreements arise, approach

discussions with empathy and a willingness to understand the other person's point of view, focusing on solutions rather than blame.

6. **Investing in Relationships**: Dedicate time and energy to nurture your relationships, whether with family, friends, or partners. Regular check-ins and shared experiences can strengthen the ties and foster a sense of community and belonging.

7. **Teaching Future Generations**: Be mindful of the legacy you leave behind. Share the principles of secure attachment with the younger generations in your life. Teach them about empathy, communication, and the importance of emotional health, empowering them to build secure connections.

By consciously implementing these practices, we can create a secure attachment legacy that enriches our lives and influences those around us. We will contribute to a culture of connection, resilience, and emotional well-being that resonates for generations.

CONCLUSION

As we conclude, take a moment to reflect on your journey. This book has been your companion in exploring the nuances of avoidant attachment, guiding you toward the possibility of secure and meaningful connections. We have delved into understanding dismissive patterns, recognizing emotional triggers, and building trust in relationships. Together, we have uncovered strategies for effective communication, emotional intimacy, and the transformative power of vulnerability. Each chapter has been a step toward dismantling the barriers that hinder deep, fulfilling relationships.

The key takeaways from this journey emphasize the importance of self-awareness and emotional literacy. Understanding your attachment style is a cornerstone of transformation. It allows you to identify and address the patterns that might have kept you distant from your desired connections. Trust-building, as we have discussed, is the foundation upon which secure relationships are built. It is about honesty, transparency, and mutual dedication to cultivating your connection with others. Emotional intimacy and effective communication are the threads that weave trust into the fabric of your relationships, fostering a deeper understanding and connection.

Reflect on your personal growth and transformation. Take a moment to recognize the significant changes in how you perceive yourself and interact with others. Every step you have taken, no matter how small, has contributed to a broader shift in how you relate to the world and those around you. Celebrate your progress and the courage it took to confront past patterns and embrace new ways of being. Your journey is a testament to your resilience and the strength within you to change and grow. You should be immensely proud of how far you have come.

Consistency and practice are vital as you continue on this path. The habits and behaviors you have developed need nurturing to become a natural part of your life. Regular reflection will keep you grounded and aware of your progress. Continuous practice will reinforce the new patterns that lead to secure attachment. Think of these practices as the gentle rain that nourishes a garden; they ensure that your growth is sustained and your relationships flourish.

Remember, the journey does not end here. Learning and self-discovery are ongoing processes essential for deepening your understanding and skills. Keep seeking out, reading, or exploring related topics that interest you. This continued exploration will enrich your journey, offering new perspectives and tools to enhance your relationships. Stay curious and open to the lessons life presents, and know that each discovery adds to the richness of your relational tapestry. Your journey is not a destination but a continuous evolution.

As you look to the future, hold on to hope and optimism. Envision a life filled with secure, fulfilling relationships. This vision is not just a dream; it is within your reach and built on the foundation of your work. The insights and strategies from this book are your guide, offering direction and support as you move forward. Allow hope to light your path, and trust in your ability to create the connections you desire.

I invite you to actively apply what you have learned daily. Share your journey and experiences with others, fostering a growth and support community. Your story can inspire others, creating a ripple effect of positive change. Together, we can build a network of people committed to understanding and overcoming avoidant attachment, creating a world where secure relationships are the norm.

Thank you for taking this transformative journey with me. Your willingness to explore and change is a testament to your courage and determination. Remember, you are not alone. Change is not only possible—it is happening within you. I offer ongoing encouragement and support as you grow and build the secure, meaningful relationships you deserve. Your journey is filled with potential for positive change, and I am confident in your ability to realize it.

The overarching goal of this book was to help you overcome avoidant attachment and build loving, secure relationships. Understanding and addressing dismissive patterns has transformative potential. You have taken significant steps toward a more connected and fulfilling life by embracing these insights. As you continue, know you have the tools and the strength to create the relationships you envision. You are capable of building the secure attachments you deserve. Embrace this journey with confidence and compassion, and let it guide you to the secure attachments you deserve.

APPENDIX: DIGITAL COMMUNICATION AND AVOIDANT ATTACHMENT

In today's interconnected world, digital communication offers opportunities and challenges for those with avoidant attachment patterns. While smartphones, social media, and instant messaging can serve as convenient shields against emotional intimacy, they also present unique opportunities for practicing vulnerability in measured, controlled ways. For individuals with avoidant attachment, these digital tools can become either a fortress reinforcing emotional distance or a bridge toward secure connection. This section explores how to recognize and transform avoidant digital patterns into opportunities for genuine connection while respecting your need for emotional safety.

MODERN TECHNOLOGY'S IMPACT ON ATTACHMENT DYNAMICS

For those with avoidant attachment, digital communication can unconsciously become a perfect tool for maintaining emotional distance. The ability to control response timing, craft careful messages, and avoid face-to-face vulnerability often reinforces avoidant patterns. While texting, instant messaging, and social media appear to facilitate connection, they can enable sophisticated forms of emotional withdrawal. Understanding how you might use these tools to maintain comfortable distance is the first step toward transforming digital habits from barriers into bridges for authentic connection.

Digital Activation Signals and Response Patterns

Understanding your digital attachment triggers is not just crucial —it is empowering. By recognizing these triggers, you gain the power to manage your online relationships effectively. Common activation signals in digital communication often manifest as emotional responses to reading receipts without responses or experiencing anxiety when encountering delayed responses to emotionally vulnerable messages. Many find themselves triggered by noticeable changes in communication patterns, whether in frequency, tone, or emojis. The visibility of social media activity without direct communication can also activate attachment concerns, as can seeing someone's online status during periods of non-response. These digital triggers often mirror in-person attachment activations but can feel more intense due to the immediate visibility of digital behavior. Developing awareness of your specific digital triggers allows for more conscious response choices rather than reactive behaviors.

TEXT COMMUNICATION AND EMOTIONAL SECURITY

Common digital avoidant behaviors include using work emails to avoid personal messages, maintaining multiple chat conversations to disperse emotional intensity, and relying heavily on GIFs or emojis to deflect from genuine emotional expression. You might also prefer text-based communication over calls, use lengthy response delays to regulate emotions or become overwhelmed when messages require emotional vulnerability. Recognizing these patterns allows you to consciously choose different responses that gradually build comfort with digital intimacy.

Digital messaging presents unique challenges for attachment dynamics. The lack of nonverbal signals, vocal tone, and physical presence can amplify attachment anxieties and avoidant tendencies. Message timing, length, and frequency often become proxy indicators for relationship security, leading to potential misinterpretations and emotional distress. However, when used mindfully, text communication can also be a tool for maintaining connection and practicing secure attachment behaviors through consistent, clear communication patterns.

Practical Strategies for Secure Digital Communication

Implementing structured approaches to digital communication can help manage attachment anxiety and build security:

1. **Time-boxing**: This is an effective strategy where you set aside specific periods for checking and responding to

messages rather than allowing anxiety to drive constant checking.

2. **Develop Thoughtful Response Templates**. These can help you navigate moments when you feel triggered but want to maintain a connection.

3. **Metacommunication**: This practice of openly discussing your digital communication style and needs proves invaluable. For instance, you might explain to a partner that you need processing time before responding to emotional messages, suggesting a specific emoji as a signal that you have read their message and will respond thoughtfully later.

Common avoidant patterns in digital communication often emerge in subtle ways. These might manifest as consistently using work to justify delayed responses or maintaining predominantly surface-level, fact-based conversations. Some individuals rely heavily on humor or deflection when conversations turn emotional, while others might withdraw entirely during periods of emotional intensity. Another typical pattern involves preferring group chats to one-on-one communication, as this creates natural emotional distance through the presence of others.

SOCIAL MEDIA'S ROLE IN MODERN RELATIONSHIPS

For those with avoidant attachment, social media can substitute for genuine intimacy, offering the illusion of connection without the vulnerability of direct interaction. The ability to maintain surface-level engagement through likes and brief comments while avoiding deeper conversations often appeals to avoidant tendencies. However, this same technology can be deliberately used to practice small acts of vulnerability, such as sharing personal thoughts or expressing appreciation for others in manageable doses.

Maintaining Digital Connection Without Dependency

Virtual relationship maintenance requires a delicate balance between staying connected and avoiding digital dependency. Regular video calls, thoughtful text messages, and shared online experiences can help maintain emotional bonds when physical presence is impossible. These digital tools are crucial in enhancing and maintaining relationships, providing reassurance and a sense of connection. However, developing strategies that complement rather than replace in-person interaction is vital. This includes establishing digital communication rituals that enhance security while respecting personal boundaries and authentic connection needs. It is important to remember that while digital tools can improve relationships, they should not replace the value of in-person interactions.

Online Resources and Virtual Support Systems

The digital age has expanded access to attachment-related support through online therapy platforms, relationship apps, and virtual support communities. These resources can provide valuable tools for understanding and improving attachment patterns, offering flexibility and accessibility that traditional support systems may lack. Online therapy sessions, in particular, can create safe spaces for exploring attachment issues while maintaining the comfort of familiar environments. However, integrating these digital resources effectively requires understanding their benefits and limitations within the broader context of attachment work.

Setting Digital Boundaries for Healthy Attachment

Establishing clear digital boundaries is essential for maintaining healthy attachment patterns in the modern age. This includes defining response expectations, managing online availability, and creating guidelines for social media engagement within relationships. Healthy digital boundaries help prevent technology from exacerbating attachment anxieties while supporting secure connections. These boundaries might include designated off-line times, agreements about public relationship sharing, and protocols for handling digital communication during conflicts. By setting and respecting these boundaries, you can create a digital environment that promotes security and respect in your relationships.

Digital Wellness and Attachment Growth

Developing digital wellness practices that foster secure attachment requires recognizing how technology shapes our relationship patterns and emotional security. This involves the mindful use of digital communication tools, regular evaluation of online interaction patterns, and adapting digital habits to support attachment objectives. By understanding the intersection of technology and attachment, individuals can utilize digital tools to enhance rather than disrupt relationship security.

Digital Connection Building Exercises

Fostering secure attachment through digital means requires intentional practice and structured approaches. Scheduled digital check-ins provide a foundation for a consistent connection. These regular interactions involve sharing meaningful aspects of your day, including successes and challenges while expressing appreciation for your relationship. This predictable structure helps build trust and security in digital communication.

Progressive digital vulnerability offers a pathway to deeper connection while respecting attachment-related fears. It is a strategy and a journey toward a more profound connection. Begin with lower-risk sharing methods, such as voice messages instead of texts, which convey more emotional nuance while maintaining some distance. Sharing photos of meaningful moments and utilizing video calls for important conversations can gradually increase intimate connection. As comfort grows, progress to real-time emotional sharing, composing digital love letters, and practicing spontaneous expressions of feelings. This journey of digital vulnerability can lead to a deeper, more meaningful connection.

Digital repair rituals are crucial for maintaining secure connections during inevitable miscommunications. Establishing clear protocols for managing digital misunderstandings helps prevent escalation and promotes repair. These include agreeing upon specific ways to signal when you need space, establishing requirements for shifting serious discussions to video calls and maintaining regular check-ins about satisfaction with digital communication patterns. These practices help build security while working toward more profound face-to-face vulnerability, remembering that digital tools should enhance rather than replace in-person connection.

INTEGRATION WITH OVERALL ATTACHMENT STRATEGY

The digital age has transformed how we experience and express attachment needs. Video calls, text messages, and social media have created new opportunities for connection while introducing novel challenges to attachment security. The instantaneous nature of digital communication can trigger attachment anxiety or avoidance in unprecedented ways.

"Digital boundaries" have become crucial in managing modern attachment challenges. This involves creating intentional practices around device use, online availability, and digital communication styles. For those with avoidant attachment, the challenge often lies in using digital tools to enhance rather than replace in-person vulnerability.

Digital communication patterns must be integrated thoughtfully into broader attachment strategies. This involves aligning online interaction styles with attachment goals, using digital tools to support rather than replace intimate connection, and maintaining awareness of how technology affects relationship dynamics. Success requires regular evaluation and adjustment of digital communication patterns to ensure they contribute positively to attachment security and relationship growth.

Consider Darla, who recognized her avoidant patterns in using digital communication. She read messages immediately but waited hours to respond, claiming work kept her busy. In group chats, she was quick with jokes and memes but would disappear when conversations turned personal. Through conscious effort, she began using digital tools differently: setting reminders to respond to individual messages within an hour, sharing one genuine feeling daily via text, and gradually increasing her comfort with video calls. While challenging, these small steps helped her transform digital communication from a shield into a bridge for authentic connection.

FURTHER READING

John Bowlby's Attachment Theory, https://www.simplypsychology.org/bowlby.html

Mary Ainsworth: Attachment Theory and the Strange Situation, https://www.attachmentproject.com/attachment-theory/mary-ainsworth/

A tangled start: The link between childhood maltreatment, psychopathology, and relationships in adulthood, https://www.sciencedirect.com/science/article/pii/S014521342100301X/

Disentangle the neural correlates of attachment style in healthy individuals, https://pmc.ncbi.nlm.nih.gov/articles/PMC6998975/

8 Attachment Style Questionnaires & Tests to Assess Clients, https://positivepsychology.com/attachment-style-tests/

Understanding Emotional Triggers and How To Handle Relationship Issues in Therapy, https://www.sunshinecitycounseling.com/blog/emotional-triggers-and-relationship-issues-in-therapy/

Mindfulness and Emotion Regulation, https://pmc.ncbi.nlm.nih.gov/articles/PMC5337506/

Dismissive Avoidant Attachment: Signs, Triggers, & More, https://www.talkspace.com/blog/dismissive-avoidant-attachment/

Cultivating Trust: 8 Essential Components for Relationship Success, https://extension.usu.edu/hru/blog/building-trust-in-relationships-guide-to-lasting-connection/

16 Exercises To Enhance Emotional Intimacy In Relationships, https://www.thewonders.com/post/16-exercises-to-enhance-emotional-intimacy-in-relationships/

Effective Communication Strategies for Couples, https://epiccounselingsolutions.com/effective-communication-strategies-for-couples-a-therapists-guide/

How Do You Fix Emotional Detachment in a Relationship? https://www.marriage.com/advice/relationship/emotional-detachment/

Conflict Resolution in Relationships & Couples: 5 Strategies, https://positivepsychology.com/conflict-resolution-relationships/

Active listening: Hear what people are really saying, https://www.mindtools. com/az4wxv7/active-listening/

Expectations in a Relationship: Reasonable vs Unrealistic, https:// anchorlighttherapy.com/expectations-in-a-relationship-a-reality-check/

How to Deal With Perfectionism in Relationships, https://www.verywellmind. com/dealing-with-perfectionism-in-a-relationship-5226092/

Secure Attachment: Signs, Benefits, Plus How to Develop It, https://www. verywellmind.com/secure-attachment-signs-benefits-and-how-to-cultivate-it-8628802/

Contributions of Attachment Theory and Research: A Framework for Future Research, Translation, and Policy, https://pmc.ncbi.nlm.nih.gov/articles/ PMC4085672/

14 Proven Ways To Build Emotional Intimacy: The Ultimate Guide In 2024, https://practicalintimacy.com/how-to-build-emotional-intimacy-relationship/

The Importance of Self Awareness in Relationships, https:// perthcounsellingandpsychotherapy.com.au/the-importance-of-self-awareness-in-relationships/

The Invisible Thread: Attachment Styles and the Therapeutic Journey in Daily Life, https://www.awakenedpathcounseling.com/attachment-styles/

Therapy for Avoidant Attachment Style, https://michaelhilgerslpc.com/avoidant-attachment-style-therapy/

Integrating Self-Help and Psychotherapy, https://academic.oup.com/book/1256/ chapter/140191997/

How Attachment Styles Impact Relationships: Healing Relational Trauma, https:// bayareacbtcenter.com/attachment-styles-relationships-relational-trauma/

Culture and Child Attachment Patterns: a Behavioral Systems Synthesis, https:// pmc.ncbi.nlm.nih.gov/articles/PMC6901642/

Culture and Child Attachment Patterns: a Behavioral Systems Synthesis, https:// pubmed.ncbi.nlm.nih.gov/31976462/

Navigating Cultural Differences in Personal Relationships: Embracing Diversity, https://medium.com/@phyllismoreau_51174/navigating-cultural-differences-in-personal-relationships-embracing-diversity-f562807c64b7/

Effective Attachment Therapy Techniques for Healing and Building Secure Relationships, https://upvio.com/nervous-system/effective-attachment-therapy-techniques-for-healing-and-building-secure-relationships/

Self-Compassion Practices, https://self-compassion.org/self-compassion-practices/

SMART goals, https://www.mindtools.com/a4wo118/smart-goals/

Understanding 4 Attachments Styles and How They Affect Adult Relationships, https://www.abundancetherapycenter.com/blog/understanding-4-attachment-styles-and-how-they-affect-adult-relationships/

Mindfulness exercises, https://www.mayoclinic.org/healthy-lifestyle/consumer-health/in-depth/mindfulness-exercises/art-20046356/

Mental Health Benefits of Journaling, https://www.webmd.com/mental-health/mental-health-benefits-of-journaling/

Mindfulness exercises, https://www.mayoclinic.org/healthy-lifestyle/consumer-health/in-depth/mindfulness-exercises/art-20046356/

Building Networks for Mental Health: A Guide, https://individualcareoftx.com/2024/04/13/building-networks-for-mental-health/

The Role of Consistency in Behavior Support Strategies, https://positivesolutionsbehaviorgroup.com/the-role-of-consistency-in-behavior-support-strategies/

The Power of Self Reflection: How to Foster Personal Growth, https://everydayspeech.com/blog-posts/general/the-power-of-self-reflection-how-to-foster-personal-growth/

The Role Of Adaptability in Relationships and Social Interactions, https://fastercapital.com/topics/the-role-of-adaptability-in-relationships-and-social-interactions.html

How to Create a Relationship Vision, https://www.lambertcouplestherapy.com/how-to-create-a-relationship-vision/